TERESA DURYEA WONG

JAPANESE

Contemporary Quilts and Quilters

THE STORY OF AN AMERICAN IMPORT

Schiffer Publishing Ltd

4880 Lower Valley Road • Atglen, PA 19310

Front cover image: Yoko Sekita, *Scheherazade*, 1994. Cotton: 36 × 41 in. (91 × 103 cm). Hand appliquéd, hand quilted.

Back cover images: *Top* Yoshiko Katagiri, 禅-*Zen* (detail), 2001. Cotton, silk antique kimono: 83 × 70 in. (212 × 178 cm). Hand appliquéd, hand quilted. *Center* Noriko Endo, *Sylvan Ambience #10* (detail), 2010. Silk, silk fiber, paint: 15 × 20 in. (38 × 50 cm). Machine embroidered, machine quilted. *Bottom* Keiko Goke, quilted balloon balls.

Title page image: Noriko Endo, *Sylvan Ambience #10* (detail), 2010. Silk, silk fiber, paint: 15 × 20 in. (38 × 50 cm). Machine embroidered, machine quilted.

Endpaper images: *Front* Makiko Aoki, *Cherry Blossoms at Night*, 2013. Cotton, tulle: 46 × 67 in. (116 × 170 cm). *Back* Noriko Endo, *Forest in New England*, 1996. Cotton, tulle: 84 × 55 in. (210 × 135 cm). Machine appliquéd and quilted.

Designed by Danielle D. Farmer
Cover Design by Brenda McCallum
Type set in BRODtwo/Zapfino/Helvetica Neue Lt Pro/Cambria

ISBN: 978-0-7643-4874-7
Printed in China

Published by Schiffer Publishing, Ltd.
4880 Lower Valley Road
Atglen, PA 19310
Phone: (610) 593-1777; Fax: (610) 593-2002
E-mail: Info@schifferbooks.com

For our complete selection of fine books on this and related subjects, please visit our website at www.schifferbooks.com. You may also write for a free catalog.

This book may be purchased from the publisher. Please try your bookstore first.

We are always looking for people to write books on new and related subjects. If you have an idea for a book, please contact us at proposals@schifferbooks.com.

Schiffer Publishing's titles are available at special discounts for bulk purchases for sales promotions or premiums. Special editions, including personalized covers, corporate imprints, and excerpts can be created in large quantities for special needs. For more information, contact the publisher.

OTHER SCHIFFER BOOKS ON RELATED SUBJECTS:

A People and Their Quilts,
John Rice Irwin, ISBN 978-0-88740-024-7

Ralli Quilts: Traditional Textiles from Pakistan and India, Patricia Ormsby Stoddard, ISBN 978-0-7643-1697-5

Amish Quilts and the Welsh Connection, Dorothy Osler, ISBN 978-0-7643-3916-5

This book is dedicated to the artists in Japan who so graciously shared their stories with me.

And to my loving husband Jimmy, who supports me in all that I do; to our children Elizabeth Ann and Christopher Kwai; and to my mother, Mary Beth Lennemann, who taught me to sew. I also dedicate this in memory of my father Eugene Jay Duryea, whose creative presence I miss dearly, and to my paternal grandmother, Frances Riley Duryea, who gave me my first quilt and so much more.

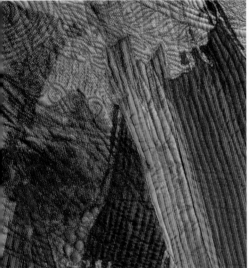

CONTENTS

ACHNOWLEDGMENTS

First and foremost, I wish to thank the artists featured here for allowing me into their homes and studios, and for sharing their stories.

I would like to acknowledge several individuals who generously offered to read drafts of this manuscript. Nancy Bailey, Ph.D., a lecturer with the Shepherd School of Music at Rice University, not only gave tirelessly of her time and talent on this manuscript, but over the years she inspired me to pursue my love of the arts. Nao Nomura, Associate Professor, Faculty of Liberal Arts at Saitama University in Japan, recommended research sources and willingly answered many questions. Polly Duryea, Ph.D., literary researcher and retired academic at University of Nebraska-Lincoln, took this manuscript to task on the places it needed it most. And quilter, former public school administrator, and friend Amy Gurghigian offered her expertise and perspective as a quilter. Mariko Akizuki and Akemi Narita both offered professional translations. I would like to acknowledge Akemi in particular for assisting me throughout this process and for accompanying me on several interviews.

I'd also like to acknowledge the support and cooperation of Noriko Endo. Noriko encourages and inspires quilters at all levels across the globe and I am especially grateful for her advice.

I would like to thank Ryoko Kobayashi, who manages the quilt section for the Japan Handicraft Instructors' Association (JHIA). Ryoko spent many months communicating with me and I appreciate her cooperation and support.

Masako Katagiri assisted with the research for this book by providing newspaper articles and translations, and she was always willing to answer a myriad of questions.

During the research process, I met with Cultural Affairs representatives from the Consulate-General of Japan in Houston, Texas, and the Embassy of the United States in Tokyo. I'd like to acknowledge their willingness to engage and thank them for sharing their views on how the arts can be used as cultural diplomacy to better relations between nations.

I also want to thank the following individuals and organizations for their support: Carolyn Ducey, Marin Hanson, Kim Taylor, and the staff at the International Quilt Study Center & Museum; Laura Lane, Marie Geary, and Pam Weeks at the New England Quilt Museum; and I would like to acknowledge the tremendous support of Karey Bresenhan, Nancy O'Bryant Puentes, Bob Ruggiero, Julie Maffei, and the Texas Quilt Museum and Quilts Inc., for their cooperation and encouragement.

Great nations write their autobiographies in three manuscripts—the book of their deeds, the book of their words, and the book of their art.

John Ruskin
1877

Mount Fuji, Japan. This iconic image has permeated artistic Japanese landscapes for centuries.

Chasing Quilts in Japan

Quilting today is both a widely expressive art form and a huge global industry. It is estimated that there are 21 million quilters in the United States and they spend roughly $3.6 billion annually on their craft. After the United States, Japan is considered the second largest concentration of quilters, with an estimated 2 to 3 million quilters.

The story is told here in two parts.

The first part tells the story of how Japanese women were initially influenced by American quilts, and how, over time, they developed their own distinct quilting styles. As is typical with such a culturally sophisticated country, Japan adopted American quilt traditions, assimilated them, and created their own aesthetic all within a span of 20 to 30 years.

The second half of the story provides an opportunity to meet the artists who are at the very heart of this transformation and see beautiful photographs of their quilts. It was a wonderful experience to seek out these artists, learn about their work and then convince them to be a part of this book. I deliberately chose a group of quilters with very different styles and techniques; no two are even remotely alike. However, each shares several distinguishing achievements: first, each is creating art that is distinctive and, in many cases, award-winning; second, each has a mature vision; third, each has perfected her art through many long years of dedication to working with needle, thread, and textiles.

My only regret is that I was not able to include the many other wonderful artists I encountered who are also doing truly important work. Publishing has limitations on space, unfortunately.

I made my first quilt in 1996. I don't ever envision a day when I will not make quilts. Inevitably, when I meet new people and explain this passion, they almost immediately launch into stories about their grandmother and the quilts she made. Like so many family stories, I also had a grandmother who quilted. She was an inspiration and I'm lucky to have one of her quilts in my collection today. My grandmother, and so many other grandmothers like her who bestowed the gift of quilting, would certainly have been thrilled to learn that the quilts they made in some ways inspired generations of women in Japan to take up their needle and thread and make their own, very special quilts.

This book shares the remarkable story of how this transformation took place. I hope that quilters and art lovers everywhere will enjoy reading it.

Note regarding names: The artists' names within this book are cited using Western style. On first reference, the given name is listed first, the surname second. On second reference, individuals are listed by their given name.

Note regarding the term patchwork: The Japanese translation for *quilt* is *patchwork*, so the term *patchwork* is used occasionally throughout this book. When referenced, *patchwork* generally applies to all quilting and is not intended in the literal Western reference of a quilt made from patches or blocks.

JAPAN'S QUILTING HISTORY

A Heavy Dose of American Influence

The Tokyo Dome is home to two iconic American imports: baseball and quilting.

Baseball, America's greatest pastime, was imported to Japan sometime around 1870. Approximately 100 years later, Japan imported another wholesome chunk of Americana: the quilt.

Once a year, these two imports unite when Tokyo's domed baseball stadium hosts the biggest quilt expo in the world where more than 230,000 attendees traipse over the baseball field to see quilts and shop for fabric, sewing machines, and all things quilt related.

This book tells the story of how an American import, the quilt, inspired a favorite pastime for an estimated three million quilters living in Japan today, and a recognizable and coveted aesthetic for the rest of the quilt world.

HUNDREDS OF YEARS OF CREATIVE EXPRESSION

For centuries, the Japanese have been perfecting the art of making textiles, dyeing them, and sewing them together. This island nation has been stitching together layers of fabric to create items such as futons, clothing, even armor and fireman's gear, for hundreds of years. Japan is also world famous for its accomplishments in fine decorative stitching techniques, such as *sashiko*.

In the decades following World War II, a generation of Japanese women began expanding their sewing skills to make quilts using styles and techniques imported from America. The explanation for how this American import took hold begins with a definition of exactly what a quilt is and how it differed from sewing techniques already present in Japan, and moves on to why these sewing enthusiasts looked to America for inspiration.

First, the definition. A quilt was originally intended to be a bedspread or coverlet, or a type of warm blanket. To fit the globally accepted criteria of a quilt, the item must have three layers: the first layer is a decorated or patchwork fabric top, the second layer is a thick material in the middle (referred to as batting), and the third layer is another textile on the bottom. These layers are stitched together and a quilt is formed.

The three-layer quilt with a decorated or patchwork top was not prevalent in Japan prior to around 1970.

Today, the definition of a quilt has vastly expanded far beyond bedspreads and includes quilts that are created as works of art meant to hang on the wall, often referred to as art quilts. The contemporary quilters featured in part two of this book are mostly making artistic quilts intended to hang on the wall.

Japan and the United States have a long and complicated diplomatic relationship, most notably dating back to the 1850s when American military officer Commodore Matthew Perry showed up uninvited on Japan's shores. Since then, a wide variety of formal and informal cultural exchanges have traveled back and forth between Japan and America.

In modern times, the Japanese have felt a special affinity for America which is stronger than connections they feel for other countries. These feelings were certainly strengthened in the post–World War II years and continue today. As recently as 2009, a government public opinion poll showed that 79% of Japanese feel close or tend to feel close to America. This statistic was significantly higher compared to any other country's result.[*]

[*]Cabinet Office of Japan Public Opinion Survey on Diplomacy, 2009. Translation courtesy of the Maureen and Mike Mansfield Foundation.

This affinity with America helps explain why some Japanese women who were already familiar with textiles and sewing looked first to the US for new ways to express themselves creatively. When they were introduced to the concept of modern quilting, these individuals quickly adopted the parts of this tradition that were new to them and blended these techniques with their own knowledge and history to create an entirely new art form.

ABOVE
Keiko Goke. *Tanabata*, 1988. Japanese cotton, linen, and synthetic fabrics: 67 × 87 in. (170 × 223 cm). Machine pieced, hand appliquéd, hand quilted.

Keiko Goke made this quilt to commemorate the brightly colored *Tanabata* festival she remembers attending while growing up in Sendai. Keiko is among the very first group of Japanese quilters to build an international reputation for innovative and original work. She was inspired early on by American quilts, especially the vibrant designs of African-American quilts.

LEFT
Yukiko Hirano. *Baltimore Album Quilt I*, 1989. Cotton: 75 × 109 in. (192.5 × 279 cm). Hand appliquéd, hand quilted. *Photo by Jim Lincoln. Courtesy of the International Quilt Association.*

Yukiko Hirano was an award-winning Japanese quilter who dedicated her life to creating quilts in the American style. This quilt pictured was the first in a long series of American Baltimore Album quilts. When she passed away in 2010, the Consulate-General of Japan in Houston and the Japanese Association of Greater Houston arranged for the donation of four Baltimore Album quilts to the permanent collection of the Texas Quilt Museum in LaGrange, Texas.

RE-EMERGENCE OF THE JAPANESE ARTS AND CRAFTS MOVEMENT: BUILDING A LAND OF CULTURE

Japan has a long history of protecting and preserving national monuments and great artistic treasures. In 1947, Prime Minister Katayama Tetsu took this concept a step further when he addressed his country after the creation of Japan's new postwar constitution and declared that Japan would be a "Land of Culture."

These words encouraged an entire nation, and especially young people, who found themselves coming of age in a more prosperous and peaceful climate than their mothers and fathers had experienced.

By the 1950s, Japan had already made the decision to preserve its tangible cultural assets such as paintings, sculpture, and architecture, but they also took the unprecedented step of preserving the intangible properties such as music, theater, and the making of crafts, which the Japanese people deemed as critical to their history.

To preserve these intangibles, the Japanese government designated a handful of people, and in some cases small groups of artisans, as "Important Intangible Cultural Properties," commonly referred to as National Living Treasures.

By 2014, the government had named 77 individuals and 26 groups as National Living Treasures. These artists are given an annual stipend (of 2 million yen) to subsidize expenses, as well as financial support to help promote their crafts through exhibitions and community outreach.

Perhaps most important to this effort are the steps taken to ensure that these National Living Treasures train their successors. Part of this effort is carried out through the country's strict *iemoto* training, which is discussed in the next chapter.

As a result of these various programs and the outreach to so many talented artisans, domestic pride swelled and Japanese society came to once again respect and revere their finely crafted traditional Japanese items such as lacquer, wood, and bamboo handicrafts, pottery and ceramics, glass products, and indigo-dyed textiles. Artisans in the 1950s also found a ready market for their handicrafts through the U.S. government, which readily accepted these soft goods as part of a payment-in-kind arrangement to fund the Allied postwar rebuilding efforts in Japan. This cultural exchange had the added benefit of helping to build better relations between the two countries.

Many exhibitions were held during these years to display these cultural goods. In addition, handicraft magazines began sprouting to share the stories of these artisans and the Japanese traditions they honored. As a result, the entire craft industry in Japan was revitalized. Society was making great strides to fulfill Japan's desire to be a "Land of Culture."

NEEDLE AND THREAD REVIVAL

A renewed interest in crafts made by needle and thread, as well as the concept of quilting as both a handicraft and a decorative art, also thrived during this extraordinary period of Japan's history. As a result, quilting as a hobby, an art form, and a career quickly flourished.

There is concrete evidence of this revival through the recollections of the quilters who were interviewed for this book, the majority of whom were born in Japan between 1930 and 1960.

Their experiences and their memories of how they were first introduced to quilting vary, but all of them agree they were either strongly influenced by, or were certainly aware of, American quilts and American quilting techniques.

Almost all of them concede that the first quilt they constructed was made in the style of a traditional American pattern, and most often it was a bedcovering. These quilters emphatically credit the American tradition over other recognizable British or Western European styles.

However, the biggest discrepancy in their recollections, and perhaps the most interesting question, is whether they were influenced by American antique quilts, as many American collectors, academics, and historians claim today, or whether they were inspired by new American quilts.

The answer to that question is as diverse as the personalities of the quilters themselves.

Some of these quilters were making quilts in Japan as early as 1970 through 1972. Others began in the mid-1980s. They were introduced to the idea of placing a layer of fabric on the top and bottom, and stuffing a layer of some sort of material in between, after they saw pictures in interior design magazines, lifestyle magazines, books, or on television. Some had special opportunities to see quilts in person, at early museum shows in Japan, or while traveling in the States.

Regardless of how they first encountered the American quilt, they were intrigued enough to try to replicate what they saw.

Sometimes these early quilts even made headlines in the local newspapers. For example, one early American-style quilt was made by members of the Japan-British Society. Their effort was forever preserved in newsprint when, on May 9, 1975, they presented their handmade quilt to Her Majesty Queen Elizabeth II during a royal visit to Tokyo. These quilters had gathered months before in anticipation of the Queen's visit and they collected fabric from their own personal, diverse fabric collections to create this large quilt.

Judging by the photo, Her Majesty looked remarkably pleased with this unique gift. The traditional quilt was created with a series of hexagon blocks interspersed with squares. The women presenting it also clearly represented the diversity of their two cultures by dressing in either traditional Japanese kimonos, or British hats and day dresses.

The chance to meet a famous Royal just doesn't come along every day, but it seems a fitting connection that a generation of women chose a newly made quilt to represent their friendship with each other and their pride in their new craft.

Other examples of this enthusiasm for quilting during these early days abound. When eager, curious women couldn't find what they were looking for in Japan, they booked flights to America. Keiko Goke, for example, recalls a quilt-related trip she made with several friends to New York, Houston, and Lancaster, Pennsylvania, as early as 1978. Yoko Saito made her first trip to the US that same year.

Some of the quilters interviewed for this book even lived in the US with their husbands and young families when their husbands accepted overseas assignments in the US.

Some quilters began collecting American antique quilts in order to appreciate their history and study the traditional sewing techniques. Others found the antique quilts boring in terms of technique and colors, so they sought out contemporary quilts.

Some found a great deal of inspiration by visiting large quilt festivals and exhibitions such as the International Quilt Festival in Houston, Texas; the Quilt National event in Athens, Ohio; and the National Quilt Museum in Paducah, Kentucky.

On May 9, 1975, during a visit to Japan, Her Majesty Queen Elizabeth is presented a quilt which was handmade by women from the Japanese-British Society. The women contributed fabric from their own collections and they dressed in their "Sunday best" to make this historic presentation: British hats and dresses and traditional Japanese kimonos. *Courtesy: The Yomiuri Shimbun ©.*

When quilting first became popular in the 1970s and 1980s, many quilters traveled to America to buy fabric and supplies, or relied on friends who did. Today, the routes between East and West are traveled back and forth equally as Japan has become a source of unique fabrics which are coveted by quilters all over the world. This photo shows the Nippori Textile Town (Fabric Town), or *Nippori Sen-i gai* district, of Tokyo. The area is home to dozens of fabric stores for quilting, fashion, and home decorating.

There are many popular stores along the Nippori Textile Town, or *Nippori Sen-i gai,* streets of Tokyo.

Nuno Works is located in the posh Roppongi Hills area of Tokyo and features high-end, designer specialty fabrics and textiles for fashion and home decorating. Many quilters seek out unique stores like this one to discover unusual and special textiles for their art quilts or fiber art creations. It is also a "destination store" for international quilters seeking fabric that is uniquely Japanese.

During these trips to the US, the quilters recall that they would purchase everything that they could feasibly carry home with them related to quilting. They bought English-language quilt books and patterns hoping to learn by studying the pictures. They bought American quilting fabrics, sometimes even batting and tools. They even bought whole quilts and quilt tops.

Once they returned home, they studied these items intently and shared them with friends or with their students. More than likely, some of the imported items were sold to those early quilters in Tokyo's first quilt store, which opened in 1976.

Some quilters didn't have to leave home to find American inspiration. They found it right in their living rooms on TV.

Japan, like many other countries, imported a great deal of American TV shows and movies during the 1970s and 1980s. Today, that scenario has flipped and the US is a huge importer of Japanese television shows, primarily anime programs which dominate broadcast programming for children and teens.

Back in 1970s Japan though, one show in particular turned out to be highly influential to a group of woman who wanted to learn to quilt. That show, oddly enough, was *Little House on the Prairie*, a Hollywood recreation of life during the pioneer days of the American Old West. The series was dubbed in Japanese. Some of the quilters interviewed for this book shared that they frequently recorded the *Little House* series on video cassettes in order to replay certain scenes. They used the pause feature to stop the recording on images of Mrs. Ingalls sitting in her rocking chair working on a quilt. So, this romanticized version of America's early pioneer days became an important source and an integral part of the education process by which Japanese quilters learned the techniques of American quilting.

American television and movies have exerted considerable influence around the world. The 1970s American television show *Little House on the Prairie* was among the long list of American programs broadcast in Japan during the 1970s and 1980s. The TV series tells a Hollywood version of the pioneer days in the American Old West through the eyes of little Laura Ingalls, played by Melissa Gilbert. Her father was played by well-known actor Michael Landon. The popular show was highly influential to quilters and other women who treasured the scenes featuring American quilts. Some quilters went so far as to videotape the shows and replay certain scenes over and over in order to study the quilts more closely.
Photographer: Silver Screen Collection.

NINETEENTH AND TWENTIETH CENTURY AMERICAN QUILTS DEBUT AT NEW YORK'S WHITNEY MUSEUM

Meanwhile, back in America, two doggedly determined art enthusiasts and collectors opened a show at the Whitney Museum of American Art in New York City in 1971 featuring 60 American quilts from their collection.

A quilt exhibition at a New York museum seems like such a normal passage of events in the modern world. However, many writers, critics, and quilt historians cite this exhibition as one of the first few examples where a museum devoted exhibition space exclusively to a show of quilts. There are at least three known prior museum exhibitions, all in the New England region, which included quilts in a significant way as part of an exhibition.

But this particular show at the Whitney Museum (1971) was the first exhibition of its kind to loudly declare that quilts were being hung and exhibited in the same fashion as paintings, and for this reason, it has attracted a lot of attention, both then and still.

At the time of the exhibition, quilt makers, art critics, patrons, academics, and art lovers were divided as to the artistic merit of the quilts on display. But with the benefit of hindsight, one thing is now undisputed. What began on the walls of the Whitney in 1971, and eventually graced the walls of museums around the world during that decade, is now considered "the" show that jump-started the movement to transform our ideas about quilt making from mere women's work into art.

These ordinary quilts, mostly collected from homes, dealers, and markets in and around New England during the late 1960s and early 1970s, were chosen to meet very specific aesthetic criteria established by the two collectors. The quilts were not chosen because of their fabrics, straight stitches, appliqué or meticulous piecing. Rather, they were valued for their use of color, the structure and form of the overall work, and most importantly, because they resembled the contemporary pop art, modern, and abstract paintings that were so prevalent in the vast majority of museum and gallery exhibitions at that time in the Western art world.

The International Quilt Study Center and Museum in Lincoln, Nebraska, is home to approximately 400 quilts from the Jonathan Holstein Quilt Collection, as well as other important historical quilts.

For the first time, quilts were taken off the bed, out of the closet, and off the rocking chair and hung in an austere museum space with white walls and subdued lighting, all for the purpose of engaging the New York art world with quilts in an entirely new way. Everything about this type of exhibition screamed "art": the tiny museum-style plaques describing the work, the advantage of distance where a viewer can step back and focus on the whole piece with no distractions from the outside world, and most notably, the stamp of an esteemed art institution defining these quilts hanging on the wall as art.

Jonathan Holstein and Gail van der Hoof were the enthusiasts who made this show a reality. They spent several years collecting the quilts that matched their specific vision, and their connections in the influential art world in New York were critical to their success in convincing the Whitney to exhibit their quilts.

Fortunately, the 1971 Whitney show was successful and the organizers went on to partner with the Smithsonian Institution, which arranged for the collection to travel to several cities in the US, and later France and England.

The exhibition that had distinctly changed attitudes about the art of quiltmaking in the Western world, was about to open up entirely new worlds to quilters and art lovers in Japan.

The International Quilt Study Center and Museum sits on the edge of the University of Nebraska campus in Lincoln, Nebraska. The center hosts exhibitions and is an important source in the quilt world for educational outreach and textile research.

In 1975, the first exhibition of the Jonathan Holstein Quilt Collection (as the quilts collected by Holstein and van der Hoof are known today) was held in February at the Shiseido art gallery in the Ginza area of Tokyo.

When people saw these antique American quilts on display in Tokyo (and later in Kyoto), what they took away were romanticized visions of frugal, hard-working American Colonial women who reused old cloth and scraps—and these notions surprised them because they differed from their concept of modern and industrialized American lifestyles.

But nonetheless, some Japanese certainly fell in love with the idea of the early American quilter and this encouraged them to think about ways to use their own scraps and other clothing, including kimonos, to make patchwork quilts of their own.

American staff from the Kyoto American Center came to Tokyo to see the Shiseido exhibition. Afterwards, they quickly approached the collectors to inquire if some of the quilts could travel to their center in Kyoto after the conclusion of the Shiseido show. The arrangements were made and a smaller group of 11 quilts left the gallery in Ginza and were sent to Kyoto.

Once people in Kyoto saw this small exhibition of American quilts, they clearly wanted to see more. What followed were arrangements to coordinate a much larger exhibition, this time with 90 quilts, to be displayed at the Kyoto Museum of Modern Art. The show *American Quilts* opened the following year, July 4, 1976, which also happened to be America's bicentennial year. Newspaper accounts of the day indicate that well over 16,000 people attended this show. It was open to the public for free the first day in honor of America's Independence Day.

Some of the contemporary Japanese quilters interviewed for this book recall that these particular quilts were an important source of inspiration. After seeing this exhibition, some of them went on to experiment, trying to replicate the quilts they had seen. This experimentation was begun rather fearlessly, without any available patterns or formal instruction. It was all trial and error.

However, it must be noted that an equal number of quilters interviewed for this book who could recall this particular show, emphatically state that while these museum shows were nice, they did not inspire them at all. Nor did they lead to the "invention" of quilting in Japan as some overly-simplistic claims purport. Some quilters believe that the Japanese quilt was already much more advanced in its creativity and techniques than what could be seen in, or learned from, antique American quilts.

The quilters interviewed go on to explain that these particular quilts from the Holstein collection were very simple, they included almost no appliqué, and their designs were plain

AMERICAN ANTIQUE QUILTS ON VIEW IN JAPAN: FROM THE HALLS OF NEW YORK TO A GALLERY IN TOKYO

A behind-the-scenes appointment reveals the archives of the International Quilt Study Center and Museum. These racks are filled with hundreds and hundreds of quilts, each carefully stored to provide the greatest chance for preservation. To study this collection is to study a portion of American history.

Unknown maker. *Rainbow Stripes* (detail), c. 1900. Made in Pennsylvania. Cotton: 73 × 81 in. (185 × 205 cm). Hand quilted. Part of the Jonathan Holstein Quilt Collection.

LEFT
Unknown maker. *ZigZag (strip elements in a chevron pattern)*, c. 1890. Made in Pennsylvania. Silk and cotton: 78 × 75 in. (198 × 190 cm). Hand quilted.

This Victorian-era crazy quilt is part of the Jonathan Holstein Quilt Collection. Many quilts in this collection were shown in Tokyo and Kyoto in 1975 and 1976. Some Japanese quilters recall that they were inspired by American antique quilts, while others found the antique quilts too old-fashioned. The author is pictured examining this quilt.

and old fashioned. In their opinion, therefore, these quilts could not attract a generation of women looking to expand their creative instincts.

Furthermore, quilts that were collected and exhibited because they resembled abstract modern paintings could not be simultaneously expected to inspire quilters to quilt, as Holstein and others have claimed since.

However, the organizers certainly deserve credit for organizing the world's first museum show featuring quilts exclusively. Their efforts were very successful when measured by museum attendance, originality, and critical reviews in newspapers of the day, and Japanese audiences by and large were certainly intrigued by what they saw.

ORDINARY QUILTS, EXTRAORDINARY COLLECTION

There are at least two seminal quilts in the collection that were part of the original Whitney show that also traveled to many international destinations. One is *Ocean Waves,* which features a block pattern that was popular in the early twentieth century. This particular quilt was made circa 1900 and it is one of the quilts cited in newspaper articles in Japan about the exhibition. Viewers likely reacted to the geometric rhythm of the strong black and white triangles, which appear offset by solid white blocks set on point. Upon closer inspection, however, the viewer will see that the black fabrics are not solid black, and the white is not solid white. Another interesting detail is that around the edges, the black fabric is replaced by a mauve-colored fabric. But rather than detract from the whole, this subtle color shift enhances the sway of the pattern.

Unknown maker. *Ocean Waves,* c. 1900. Vermont. Cotton: 78 × 96 in. (198 × 243 cm). Hand quilted.

This beautiful antique quilt is made in the popular pattern known as ocean waves. Typically these quilts feature blue and white fabrics, but instead of blue this one features soft black cotton prints and mauve, rust, and pink fabrics on the outer edges. The author is pictured here (right) with Kim Taylor, IQSCM collections manager.

INSPIRATION FROM VINTAGE AFRICAN-AMERICAN QUILTS

Some contemporary Japanese quilters were strongly influenced by vintage African-American quilts from the late nineteenth and early twentieth centuries.

The vivid, bold color combinations and the improvisational piecing employed in the African-American quilts at that time were a distinct departure from the soft colors and precise, repetitive patterns of other American quilts. The folk art appeal and daring color choices seen in these quilts were especially inspiring to those Japanese quilters who were searching for ways to expand their views of quiltmaking.

During the late 1990s and 2000s, Japanese quilters seeking diverse art forms would have had numerous opportunities to discover African-American quilts through magazine articles, quilt books, and museum exhibitions.

For example, some quilters who traveled frequently to the US recall having the opportunity to see the widely-celebrated museum exhibition of African-American quilts known as *The Quilts of Gee's Bend*, which opened in 2002, featuring African-American quilts from the tiny town of Gee's Bend, Alabama. This exhibition was curated by the Museum of Fine Arts, Houston, and it traveled to a dozen cities throughout the US.

While the *Gee's Bend* exhibition showcased unique quilts from just one small community, there was an American artist and collector who spent several decades quietly building a significant collection of vintage African-American quilts from farms, small towns, and cities all over the South. Most of the quilts in her collection were made in the early twentieth century, but a few date back to the late nineteenth century.

The collector, Corrine Riley, eventually amassed a sizable quantity of quilts and her collection began to draw the attention of academics and curators who were seeking to showcase the often overlooked efforts of African-American quilters.

In 2007, part of the collection of Corrine Riley was brought to Tokyo and exhibited at the Shiseido Gallery in Tokyo. Interestingly, this contemporary art gallery is operated by the same organization that hosted the first exhibition of antique American quilts in 1975.

These colorful African-American quilts were a world apart from the gentle colors, tidy stitches, and super-straight seams typically seen in most Japanese quilts of the day.

These vintage and culturally unique quilts continue to draw attention. In 2011, the Mingei International Museum in San Diego, California, published a book with Corrine Riley featuring some of the finest African-American examples from her collection. The book is appropriately titled *Bold Expressions*.

Inside the Shiseido Gallery in the Ginza area of Tokyo during the 2007 exhibition of African-American quilts from the Collection of Corrine Riley.
Courtesy: Collection of Corrine Riley.

What began as a resurgence in traditional Japanese handicrafts became intermingled with a fascination with American quilts—both old and new. Over the next four decades, intercultural exchanges between the two countries resulted in a mature, artistic Japanese product that is now coveted by, and exported, to a global quilting audience.

Unknown maker. *Strip Quilt*, c. 1940–1950. East Texas. Cotton ribbed fabric, flour sack backing: 66 × 84 in. (167 × 213 cm). Hand quilted. *Courtesy: Collection of Corrine Riley.*

Featured in a 2007 exhibition in Tokyo of African-American quilts, this bold, modern design was appealing to contemporary Japanese quilters.

In 2007, the Shiseido Gallery in the Ginza area of Tokyo hosted an exhibition of African-American quilts from the Collection of Corrine Riley. In 1975, the Shiseido company also hosted the first exhibition of American antique quilts ever shown in Japan. *Courtesy: Collection of Corrine Riley.*

CHRONOLOGY

1950196019701980199020000s The American quilt made its way to Japan gradually in various ways from 1950 through the 1980s. Most people credit the 1970s as the pivotal decade in this journey. This timeline describes some of the most widely understood ways the Japanese absorbed American quilts and quilting.

American missionary women, along with the wives of American military officers and expatriate American businessmen, teach their Japanese friends and neighbors quilting techniques.

American quilting books and patterns are imported or purchased and shared. These publications include home decorating books and lifestyle magazines that featured quilts.

Formal cultural exchanges between Japan and the US encourage both a resurgence in Japanese handicrafts and a heightened interest in American arts and crafts, including needlework.

Blanchette and John D. Rockefeller III visit Japan (1951) with the intention of boosting the domestic arts and crafts movement. Japanese handicrafts are used as payment-in-kind to American and Allied forces throughout the 1950s to help fund the rebuilding effort.

Rockefeller reopens the Japan Society (a cultural organization that had folded prior to World War II) in order to bring the United States and Japan closer together and support cultural exchanges.

American Quilts, an exhibition of antique American quilts, is exhibited at the Shiseido Gallery in Tokyo, and at the Kyoto American Center (1975). This is the first exhibition of American quilts in Japan. These quilts were collected from the New England states by Gail van der Hoof and Jonathan Holstein and were chosen because they resembled abstract modern-art paintings that were popular in the New York art scene at the time.

Quilts from this same collection return for an exhibition at the National Museum of Modern Art in Kyoto (1976).

Sanki Nohara and his wife, Chuck, open Japan's first quilt school, Hearts & Hands Patchwork Quilt School in Tokyo (1976). The majority of the curriculum is based on American quilt making traditions and patterns.

Japan's first retail quilt store, Quilt House Yama, opens in Tokyo (1976).

America in Patchwork, a collection of nineteenth-century American quilts, is exhibited at the Seibu Museum of Art in Tokyo (1977).

Japanese quilters make pilgrimages to the US to buy books, fabric, tools, and whole quilts. Keiko Goke and five friends are among this first wave (1978). Yoko Saito also makes her first visit to the US the same year (1978).

Sanae Hattori opens Sanae Art Studio to teach quiltmaking using Japanese classical designs and American patchwork techniques (1978).

American television shows, most notably the series *Little House on the Prairie*, are highly influential and become a source for quilters to see and replicate quilts.

1950s–1960s | 1970s

The following exhibitions of American quilts are shown in Japan:

> Curator Sandi Fox: exhibition of quilts from the collections of Margaret Maddox Cavigga (1981) and quilts from the Pilgrim Roy Collection (1983–1984).

> Curator Kei Kobayashi: exhibition of quilts from the Shelburne Museum in Vermont (1985).

> Curator Takako Onoyama: two exhibitions of quilts from the Denver Art Museum (1986, 1989).

> Antique patchwork quilts from the Spencer Museum at the University of Kansas (1987).

Margaret Maddox Cavigga (with Chuck's Patchwork School as editor) publishes a volume on American antique quilts (1981). Kei Kobayashi publishes an encyclopedia of American quilts (1983). Both volumes are in Japanese.

Yoko Saito opens her school and retail store, Quilt Party, in Tokyo (1985). Thirty years later, this business is among the most successful quilt businesses in the international quilt world.

Japanese quilters continue visiting the US to seek out antique quilts, modern quilts, and vintage African-American quilts. They bring home new ideas and techniques seen in both antique and modern quilts to incorporate into their work.

Japanese quilters attend quilt events in Athens, Ohio; Paducah, Kentucky; and Houston, Texas.

First book with a definitive survey of Japanese quilts is published in English by Jill Liddell and Yuko Watanabe (1988).

Japan Handicrafts Instructor Association (JHIA) and *Asahi Shimbun* newspaper organize *World Quilt Festival* in Tokyo (1988). Response is tremendous: ~175,000 people attend.

Buoyed by the success of *World Quilt Festival*, JHIA hosts its first juried quilt exhibition, *Quilt Nihon* (1989–1990). American Michael James is invited as a judge.

New York's American Folk Art Museum hosts one of the first international exhibitions of a selection of quilts from Japan as part of the *Great American Quilt Festival 2* curated by Donna Wilder (1989).

Kumiko Sudo is invited to teach at the International Quilt Festival in Houston, Texas (1987). She is the first Japanese instructor selected for this opportunity to teach at the biggest quilting event in the United States. Two years later, Emiko Toda Loeb also begins teaching in Houston (1989).

Jinny Beyer, Kaffe Fassett, Libby Lehman, Roberta Horton, and other quilt instructors from the West begin traveling to Japan (late 1980s) to share their modern techniques and style. They teach numerous classes and workshops throughout Japan.

1980s

Hearts & Hands Patchwork Quilt School hosts multiple quilt festivals which include exhibitions of a variety of American quilt styles: Amish, Hawaiian, New York, etc. These displays are curated by Victoria Hoffman and other organizers, and also include notable quilts from the American Folk Art Museum.

Made in Japan: American Influence on Japanese Quilts is curated by Kei Kobayashi and exhibited in several U.S. cities (1990). This is the first original museum exhibition of contemporary quilts curated (not juried) from Japanese quiltmakers. New England Quilt Museum in Lowell, Massachusetts, is the first venue.

Japan takes center stage at the annual International Quilt Festival in Houston (1990) as a 40-foot (12-meter) quilt designed by Akio Kawamoto and stitched by 1,400 Japanese quilters hangs from the ceiling of the convention center. A special exhibition, *Beauty in Japanese Quilts*, is also on view.

Kei Kobayashi organizes multiple "quilt destination" tours of New England. More than 300 Japanese participate over a 10-year period.

International Quilt Week Yokohama launches. It begins under another name (1992) and relocates to the port city of Yokohama (1995). The show includes a juried competition of quilts, and a large retail expo.

Nihon Vogue and JHIA expand their international outreach by sponsoring a special award category within both the American Quilt National (Athens, Ohio) and Quilt Visions (San Diego) competitions (1995 to present). The award is named "Quilts Japan Prize."

International Quilt Study Center and Museum at the University of Nebraska-Lincoln exhibits quilts from the Robert James Collection at the Tokyo International Forum (1998).

1990s

The first Tokyo International Great Quilt Festival opens at the Tokyo Dome (2002). In 2014, more than 237,000 people attend this annual event.

One Hundred Japanese Quilts: An Exhibition of New Works by Quilt Artists in Japan is organized by JHIA and Kokusai Art (2002) and travels throughout Japan, the US, and Europe. A catalog featuring the 100 quilts and their makers is published.

Japanese Imagery in One Hundred Quilts is a second collection of 100 quilts organized by JHIA and Kokusai Art (2004). This exhibition also travels throughout Japan. A catalog is published.

Vintage African-American quilts from the collection of Corrine Riley are exhibited at the Shiseido Gallery in Tokyo (2007).

Noriko Endo is the first Japanese quilter to win "Best of Show" at Quilt National (2007), an international competition hosted in the US.

2000s

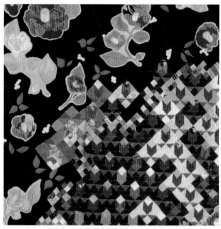

Yoshiko Katagiri. 大—Yuttari (Peaceful) (details).

TOP LEFT
Ikuko Fujishiro. *A Feeling of Love*, 1991. Antique silk kimono fabric: 86 × 98 in. (220 × 250 cm). Hand quilted.

Ikuko Fujishiro began quilting in 1976 and she was a true quilting pioneer. She was among the first to make exclusive use of antique silk kimono fabric in pieced quilts and by so doing, she created quilts that were contemporary but also honored traditional Japanese textiles.

BOTTOM LEFT
Yoshiko Katagiri. 大—Yuttari (Peaceful), 2014. Cotton, silk antique kimono: 93 × 65 in. (235 × 165 cm). Hand appliquéd, hand quilted.

LEARNING TO QUILT IN JAPAN

Two Schools of Thought

LEARNING INSIDE THE *IEMOTO* SYSTEM

The term that is widely used to describe the traditional Japanese quilt instruction system is *iemoto*. *Ie* can be translated as house, or household, and *moto* means origin or root.

Therefore, the term *iemoto* can be loosely translated to mean a charismatic master teacher, or head of the household, who gives instruction based on strict training, repetition, and the quest for flawless art. The *iemoto* system refers to a set of traditions that are recognized and widely understood in Japanese society. The artisans and instructors and benefactors involved in this system of instruction go to great lengths to ensure these traditions are formally preserved.

Traditional arts such as theater, tea or incense ceremonies, flower arranging, martial arts, poetry, and other cultural arts follow the *iemoto* system and as a result, they are guaranteed preservation. The *iemoto* system bestows certain rights and obligations on each generation in order to preserve the art form and to keep its creation process occurring in the same way it has always been done. Quilting instructors appropriated parts of the *iemoto* model for their own teaching methods when they began offering quilt instruction in the late 1970s.

When a student takes instruction under *iemoto* training, he or she begins a longterm relationship whereby they are given the right to learn and eventually perform the technical artistry and cultural traditions they have been taught. Essentially, they are gifted trade secrets. After many years of dedicated study, qualifying students are granted certificates to transmit, and teach, this same craft to the next generation, thereby preserving the art as well as the whole system.

The major tenets of the *iemoto* system are preservation and standardization.

Individual students within the *iemoto* system can expect to progress through different levels of instruction by proving they are capable of a certain level of mastery of standardized skills for that particular level. If qualified, they continue progressing through the system, and once they prove they are capable, they are certified as masters: instructors who are worthy of sharing this specialized knowledge.

For those who advocate for this type of system, these certificates are highly valued, and students invest heavily, spending both time—years, in fact—and of course money, to obtain them.

In 1969, when the predecessor to the Japan Handicraft Instructors Association (JHIA) was formed, its primary purpose was to provide instruction and training for those seeking the pursuit of handicrafts such as knitting, lacework, and embroidery. The quilt section (or patchwork section, as it is referred to in Japan) of JHIA was formed in 1986.

Nobuaki Seto, Chairman of JHIA and the son of the organization's founder, Tadanobu Seto, explains that Japanese people value authorized certifications for their accomplishments, and therefore, as JHIA raised the standards for instruction in these arts, it simultaneously established strict criteria for certifying individuals deemed qualified to teach other students.

In this way, JHIA ensures quality throughout the whole system, and its efforts have the backing of the Japanese government which assesses and approves the JHIA methods and curriculum.

There are also other large, private enterprise instruction programs within Japan that follow similar curriculum and certification models.

The following is a simplified example of the JHIA quilting curriculum. It can be compared to achieving a black belt in martial arts: there are numerous levels, each to be mastered before one advances to the next.

The first level is "basic." Curriculum at this level will require approximately six months of training at a minimum. Students will be expected to complete dozens of patterns, quilts and other assignments. This work must be presented to the instructor and approved by him or her. These assignments must be deemed acceptable to move on the next level. A certificate is awarded upon completion of this basic level.

The next level, "advanced," requires a minimum of an additional six months of training. To finish this level requires mastering a new set of more challenging skills and completing a large number of assignments and quilts to demonstrate that mastery. An advanced certificate is awarded upon completion.

After this, the student can progress to the "instructor" level which requires an additional twelve months of training, minimum. As you would expect, this level has an increasingly difficult workload and is subject to the same assessment requirements in order to proceed. An instructor certificate is awarded upon completion.

A person can only become an official member of JHIA after completing all of these courses and obtaining the "instructor" level certification.

Following the instructor level, one can continue advancing by attempting additional training to reach the "professional" status. This highest level is rewarded with further certification.

By 2014, approximately 7,000 quilt instructors were certified members of JHIA. The vast majority of their instructors reside in Japan, but some live in Taiwan, Korea, Thailand, and elsewhere.

When most of these instructors reach this highly-valued level of certification and membership, they return to their communities and begin a career as a quilt instructor. Some even open quilt shops.

The instruction these new JHIA instructors offer their students will follow this same system of rigorous study and repetition of basic skills they themselves have mastered, thereby preserving the fundamental principle of the *iemoto* system.

The *iemoto* quilt instruction model emphasizes quality first and foremost, and in Japan, that means the ability to work by hand. Not just any level of handwork will do—only the tidiest and most accurate hand stitches are allowed.

This emphasis on working by hand and this system of rigorous training is unique to Japan.

As a result, the overall level of technical artistry and pure creative accomplishment in the hand appliqué, hand stitching and hand quilting of Japanese quilts is extraordinary. It is also one of the tangible elements of the Japanese aesthetic that is now instantly recognizable to the global quilt world.

GOVERNMENT-SANCTIONED QUILT INSTRUCTION

Yoko Sekita. *Spring Midnight* (detail), 2013. *Nishijin-ori* obi textiles, silk, cotton: 51 × 74 in. (130 × 188 cm). Hand appliquéd, hand quilted.

Through her rich narrative style, Yoko Sekita features opera singers and other theatrical players as they begin to party at the stroke of midnight, exposing their playful side that theatergoers would never see. Her quilt is rich in detail and tells the story of a humorous slice of life in the wee hours of the night.

THE *IEMOTO* CLASSROOM

The most noticeable difference between the classroom instruction within the *iemoto* system and typical instruction in the West is that these students are situated in a formal classroom setting. The instructor lectures, the students sit.

The instructor is often situated at the head of the classroom marking on a chalkboard or showing examples of patterns or quilted pieces, and the students listen intently and take notes. There is rarely hands-on sewing or interaction. There are typically no sewing machines.

The instruction itself is very specific, with little room for ambiguities. This puts a lot of pressure on the instructor to create course material for each lesson that is clearly communicated and creative enough to stimulate the students. The instructor also must review the students' projects and provide formal feedback. Some schools even provide feedback in a form similar to a school report card.

The other incredibly important difference about this type of instruction is that the student typically receives instruction from this master teacher for many, many years, sometimes for the rest of their life. There is an unwritten agreement between teacher and student that they will enter into a relationship that typically lasts five years at minimum. In reality, it is typical for a student to take lessons for 20 years or more from the same teacher! Under this system, breaking away from that teacher can, in fact, be problematic in terms of the student's future reputation within Japan's quilt community.

The students are cognizant of these facts going into the arrangement. They study different methods and teaching styles before selecting an iemoto course, and make their decision based on their research.

HEARTS & HANDS PATCHWORK QUILT SCHOOL: JAPAN'S FIRST QUILT INSTRUCTION

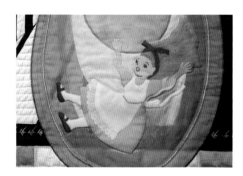

Miki Murakami. *Alice's Kitchen* (detail). 2011.

Alice falls through the teardrop. Her figure is made with hand embroidery and is hand appliquéd. The teardrop is covered with a soft layer of pale green organza.

The Hearts & Hands Patchwork Quilt School founded by Sanki Nohara and his wife, Chuck, opened in 1976. This formative institution was located in Tokyo and it was the first serious training available for quilters. It was structured as an *iemoto* school.

The husband-wife team expanded their schools to several cities beyond Tokyo, and by 1981 they operated 11 schools throughout Japan. Sanki Nohara passed away in 1990 and the school was later renamed Chuck's Quilt School with Chuck Nohara.

Many quilters who are still actively making quilts today fondly credit Hearts & Hands, and both Sanki and Chuck Nohara, for encouraging them and helping create careers in the quilting arts.

As the first school of its kind, Hearts & Hands preceded the establishment of the patchwork section in JHIA. In fact, the success of this school paved the way for JHIA to build its own curriculum and certification program a decade later.

For Hearts & Hands, and the many other instructors and schools that followed in its path, the formal study of American quilt patterns and blocks was a significant part of their curriculum during these early years.

Many students recall hours and hours of repetitive study, some say even years, making American quilt blocks and patterns in these schools. In some cases they only worked from pictures because there was no Japanese translation available.

Mariko Akizuki recalls visiting Hearts & Hands on countless mornings during the early 1980s on the way to her regular, full-time job, in order to help the owners translate articles, patterns, and quilt instructions from English into Japanese. Mariko had lived in the US for several years in the mid-1970s and she also learned to quilt during that time. The combination of her English skills, plus her thorough knowledge of quilting, made her a very capable professional translator in the quilt world. Years later, she even eventually began offering quilt instruction herself.

At the same time that Hearts & Hands was formed, Takako Onoyama opened Quilt House Yama, Japan's first retail quilt store. The store was located in Tokyo and its opening day was March 10, 1976. Many quilters recall visiting this store frequently in its early days.

In 1978, Takako Onoyama made the first of many trips to the US to learn machine quilting and to study Western retail operations. In fact, she befriended and was later mentored by Jewel Pearce Patterson and her daughter Karey Patterson Bresenhan. The two Americans operated a popular quilt store in Houston, Texas, for several decades, and Karey is one of the co-founders of the International Quilt Festival in Houston.

These fruitful connections, coupled with her new knowledge of American quilting techniques, tools, and notions, were beneficial to her business. Of course, as the first such retail business of its kind in Japan, she also faced many challenges.

For example, when it first began operations, Quilt House Yama had a difficult time importing goods from the US, so most of the fabrics the store originally sold were textiles that Takako either dyed or made herself. Most assuredly, Takako also faced obstacles due to the store being a woman-owned business during a time when most commercial enterprises in Japan were dominated by men.

But she persevered and over the years, she arranged for many U.S. quilt instructors to come to Japan and teach classes at her store. Between 1990 and 1995, she spearheaded a major effort that offered quilting classes to over 100,000 individuals in Japan.

JAPAN'S FIRST RETAIL QUILT STORE

Reiko Kato owns the quilt school and shop Mother's Dreams, and her business falls into the category of a modern version of the *iemoto* system.

She's been teaching since 2000, and most of her current students have been with her for at least eight to ten years. Some students live several hours away and commute to her school at least once a month for instruction. Mother's Dreams is located in Edogawa-ku, Tokyo.

Reiko has over 100 students and she personally teaches 20 days a month. As is expected of her, the curriculum she gives to her students is strict and well organized, and like the *iemoto* system she emulates, she offers varying phases of instruction and certification for achieving certain levels. Her quilt school focuses on handwork.

MOTHER'S DREAMS: AN EXAMPLE OF A MODERN *IEMOTO* SCHOOL

Reiko Kato is the owner of Mother's Dreams, a quilt school and store located in Edogawa, Tokyo. Reiko is a popular instructor and quilter, and is the author of several books.

This class of three students is being taught by Reiko Kato at her studio, store, and school Mother's Dreams in Tokyo. This class setting is typical of the *iemoto* system of instruction where a master teacher lectures and students listen intently and take notes. These quilters will be expected to master certain skills and complete a number of projects in order to progress upwards. Certificates are awarded for each level.

The handwork, motif, and colors of these quilted purses are representative of the traditional techniques taught at Mother's Dreams.

These three-dimensional quilted pieces are a creative extension of the typical quilt.

In the basic class, students learn to make 48 quilts in two to four years. Each project is submitted to the instructor, who reviews it and offers feedback. Reiko keeps her class size small, about 6 or 7 students per session, primarily because the classroom in her quilt store is fairly small. She also prefers a smaller class size.

The second level of her instruction is an advanced class where students learn to make an additional 48 quilts.

Once this level has been mastered, her last class is a master level and the students at this level are encouraged to create a certain number of quilts of their own pattern and design. These quilts and other sewing projects are also turned in to the instructor for evaluation.

It is after this class, and approximately five years of study, that some of Reiko's students then become instructors themselves.

One of the things her students like most about the Mother's Dreams school is the fact that Reiko regularly coordinates exhibitions of their work. Every 12 to 18 months, in fact, she hosts an exhibition at a selected gallery in Japan, and even at international venues.

For example, in 2013, her students' work was featured in a special exhibition at the International Quilt Festival in Houston, Texas.

Beyond teaching, Reiko has also achieved a certain amount of success in sharing her expertise through the six books she has published to date. Three of them are in Japanese and three completely different books have been published in French. She has also published patterns for quilts, purses, and other small items in Japanese, English, French, and Chinese.

She does not compete in quilt competitions, because she only wants to make quilts for enjoyment. Still, she is often invited to be a guest speaker at quilt events in Japan. In addition, she is featured frequently in the international quilt magazine *QuiltMania*, which is published in France. She also travels regularly to France and other European countries to teach workshops and classes.

Today, the most common form of instruction through the formal *iemoto* system focuses on traditional handwork, a skill that is highly valued in Japan. This handwork most typically means the appliqué, piecing, and quilting are done by the quilter's hand—no machines are used. Typically, the quilter will construct the pieces and complete the quilting stitches while the quilt sits on her lap, and sometimes it is secured using a large hoop or frame.

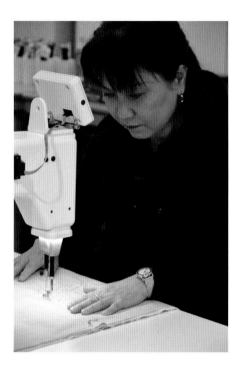

Visually, there is an obvious distinction between hand-quilted and machine-quilted stitches. The hand-quilted stitch is formed with just one piece of thread and as the needle is inserted in and out, there will be a tiny space between each stitch. The machine stitch uses two threads, one on the top and another on the bottom. As a result, the stitching is continuous. There are no spaces between each stitch.

Even though handwork is very popular in Japan, it is a misconception to assume that machine work, and free motion quilting, is not popular as well. In fact, the preference for free motion quilting is growing rapidly and the majority of quilters interviewed for this book are machine quilters. Some have been working exclusively on the machine for twenty years or more.

This student is learning to free motion quilt. Free motion quilting has been popular in Japan since early 2000 and some contemporary quilters have been using this technique for much longer. Modern sewing machine manufacturers now offer a wide variety of high-end machines in Japan for home use.

JAPAN'S FIRST SEWING MACHINES

The first wave of sewing machines imported to Japan were made in Germany and Great Britain. But by the early 1900s, the sturdy American-made Singer sewing machine was imported to Japan, and it quickly became the most popular imported sewing machine.

Once those machines were in use, they needed repairs and maintenance. In 1908, Kanekichi Yasui started a sewing machine repair business to service these imported machines. This young business was successful, but Kanekichi's son, Masayoshi, wanted to do more.

He saw an opportunity for Japan to invent and build a sewing machine that would be equal to, or better, than those made in other parts of the world. He also wanted to turn around the notion that Japan was merely an importer and he wanted to see his machines exported, and in demand, around the world.

He succeeded, and Masayoshi Yasui, along with his brother Jitsuichi, created the Brother Group, which today is a huge, diversified company that creates and manufactures sewing machines, printers, home office technology, and many other products and services.

The Brother company built and sold their first home sewing machine in 1932 and their first machine targeted to quilters, called the Quilt Club, was sold in 1994. The Quilt Club was launched in Japan first, and then Brother began exporting it to the US, UK, and Europe. Today, there are dozens of types of Brother sewing machines, sergers, and embroidery machines on the market and the brand is widely recognized by quilters everywhere.

Also during the early part of the twentieth century, another enterprising individual in Japan, Yosaku Ose, started up the Pine Sewing Machine Factory in 1921. This company invented and manufactured a line of domestic sewing machines and they were so successful that the company went on to become the Janome Sewing Machine Company.

Students often keep journals with samples of their machine quilted work.

Janome still creates innovative domestic machines that are sold throughout Japan and all over the world. Janome introduced its first highly-specialized quilter's machine in the US in 2002, and then began selling it in Japan a year later.

It turns out that the 1920s and 1930s were critical decades for the sewing industry in Japan because at the same time that Yosaku Ose and Masayoshi Yasui were building new sewing machine factories, another entrepreneur began making and selling twisted silk yarns and thread that were vital to the kimono and sewing industries.

At the time, silk was very expensive and many dealers often "shorted," or cheated, their customers when selling silk yarn by weight. But the founders of Fujix, a high-quality Japanese thread company that opened for business in 1921, took a different route. They guaranteed the weight of their precious silk products from day one and they printed labels stating that the weight of their silk was strictly guaranteed.

This early focus on quality and building the customer's trust still pervades the company's culture today. Nearly a century later, Fujix remains a thriving business and a vital part of the Japanese quilting industry. The company introduced their first thread products exclusively for quilting in 1989 and they offer a wide variety of silk and polyester threads for both hand and machine quilting.

Fujix, Janome, Brother, and other brands from Asia, North America, and Europe of course, continue innovating and introducing newer and more sophisticated threads and machines for home use that are marketed specifically for quilters.

In the mid-2000s, the Japanese manufacturers gathered together in order to support this growing interest in sewing arts. They formed the Japan Sewing Machine Manufacturers Association and this group contributes machines and other services to support sewing and other needle art classes all over Japan. They also help educate quilters specifically about the benefits and techniques of creating quilts by machine.

These technical innovations created specifically for quilting include computerized mechanisms for better stitch regulation and Internet connected machines for quilters to download patterns, specialty stitches, and such.

Manufacturers also continue to improve the most vital function for quilters, and that is the way the machines allow quilters to sew in any direction, also known as free motion sewing. Free motion works by disengaging the feed dogs, which are the mechanisms intended to propel the cloth forward or backward. This allows the sewist to stitch a creative design by moving the quilt under the needle in any direction desired.

These specialized quilting machines also have customized features such as a knee-lift bar that allows the sewist to use a knee to lift the needle and foot, so the hands can continue to hold the fabric in place.

In 2006, JHIA added instruction in machine quilting to its curriculum which has further added to the popularity of free-motion quilting and sewing.

LIFE FAR OUTSIDE THE *IEMOTO* SYSTEM: NORIKO ENDO AND KEIKO GOKE

Outside of the formal system, there exists an entirely alternate world of quilt instruction that is gaining momentum. These classes are hands-on and students sew, cut fabric, assemble quilts, and create textile collages and other works of art. The emphasis here is on innovation, on doing, and on free motion quilting on the machine.

In these situations, award-winning Japanese quilters are teaching classes in Japan that are structured more like classes one would teach in America, Europe, the UK, or Australia.

These teachers are entrepreneurial in their approach and while some of them may hold college degrees, they are not certified under JHIA or another *iemoto* system. This is perfectly acceptable to them, and in some cases even preferred.

The instructor can be found offering suggestions or providing a specific project to work on, but then the lecture, or instruction, ends and the students go to work at their own pace. The instructor will move about the room and check in with students to offer guidance or encouragement. In other settings, students bring their own projects and receive feedback, encouragement, and suggestions during the class period from their teacher.

Noriko Endo offers numerous classes in this manner in Tokyo, and all over the world. But in Japan, like Reiko Kato, she has students who have studied with her for many years. Some of Noriko's students are so dedicated that they are willing to travel all night, sometimes ten hours by bus, in order to arrive in Tokyo in the morning in time for one of her classes.

Students in classes such as these typically sit at state-of-the-art "long arm" machines or modern domestic sewing machines and work on projects. With a long arm machine the quilt is held taut and stationary on a frame and the sewing machine portion is positioned on an arm so it can move freely over a large area.

Students who train outside the iemoto system are well aware that they are getting a very different perspective and they have chosen to study with Noriko and teachers like her for many reasons.

In Noriko's case, students are first inspired by her body of work and they want to learn from her and emulate her techniques. Second, they find her creative energy and willingness to push them in entirely new directions motivating. And third, they feel that by associating with a modern, master teacher who is recognized internationally, they are positioning themselves for the best instruction available, regardless of the fact that she is not certified under JHIA to instruct and they will not be granted certificates in her classes.

Keiko Goke is also a long-time instructor, and like Noriko, she is a self-taught artist and is not certified by any organization to teach or grant certificates. Frankly, such an idea would be completely foreign to Keiko, given her independent style and innovative quiltmaking techniques.

When she first began quilting (around 1970), the idea was so novel that she was featured in a local newspaper article in Sendai, in northern Japan, where she lives. Afterwards, she was approached by several people in the community who wanted to learn to quilt, and so, thinking it might be fun to teach, she began offering instruction. Eventually,

Students in this classroom are learning to free motion quilt in a setting very similar to the way quilt classes would be taught in the West. The instructor, Noriko Endo, starts the class with a short lecture or explanation, then the students go to work at their own pace. The instructor will walk around the room and provide additional explanation and encouragement. These quilters are working on HandiQuilter Sweet 16 machines which are provided to this class for the day. This machine differs from other domestic quilt machines because it is oriented to face the sewer. For some quilters, this makes it easier to control the fabric and sew large quilts because there is ample room for the fabric behind the needle.

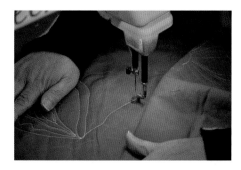

This close-up shows the free motion sewing foot in action. The quilter will move the fabric in any direction she chooses, thus the term "free motion." In this example, her design is pre-marked in chalk on the quilt top.

as her students progressed, Keiko began coordinating exhibitions of their work to share the art of quilting with her community.

Initially Keiko did not charge these beginning quilters for this instruction, but after several years, the women felt they should be compensating Keiko for all the time she was spending with them. At first she just laughed at the idea, but they insisted, so she finally agreed to accept a small monthly fee.

In order to build her reputation and further her teaching capabilities, she decided to enter international competitions and use success in that world as an indication of her talent and skill. In 1989 and 1991, she was awarded top prizes in the first and second Quilt Nihon exhibitions (see chapter 4) and one of her art quilts was accepted into the 1991 Quilt National competition hosted in the US.

So, her strategy worked, and some 30 years later she is still teaching. She has many students who have been with her for decades, and she has at least one student who has been with her since the very beginning.

When asked if she has raised her prices over the years, Keiko finds the question amusing. It is interesting to note that if Keiko Goke were teaching a class in America for $30 to $50 a month, her studio would be flooded with applicants. Oddly enough, even though she has won a great many international awards, has had a long and successful career as a fabric designer, and has published six books, she is not overwhelmed with teaching requests from inside Japan.

One explanation might be that many emerging quilters, or beginning Japanese students, are either afraid or unwilling to approach her for lessons because they most likely consider her skill as above theirs in the quilt world hierarchy. In Japanese culture, it is important to know your place in society and to respect, or at least acknowledge, these social differences between master and student.

So rather than approach her directly, these beginning students might approach one of Keiko Goke's students for instruction. The term "student" in this case refers to quilters who most likely have been associated with Keiko Goke for 20 years or more and the vast majority are master quilters themselves. Keiko suggests her students are more creative than her, and that she learns as much from them as she teaches.

MIKI MURAKAMI: FROM KEIKO GOKE STUDENT TO MASTER QUILTER

Sometime around 2001, Miki Murakami decided she wanted to learn to quilt. In order to find a teacher, she took the modern route and typed "quilt" into the search engine on her computer. She landed on the vivid artwork of Keiko Goke and she was bold enough to approach her for lessons. She began with an intensive crash course in quilting, called *quilt juku*, taught by Keiko and sponsored by Nihon Vogue Publishing Company.

Miki must have been meant to study with Keiko because she quickly made Keiko's intense and lively color palette her own. She credits Keiko's encouragement and mentorship for much of her success as a quilter today. In fact, she describes Keiko as a fantastic coach, which seems an apt term for this modern teacher-student relationship.

Miki Murakami is now an award-winning quilter. Her many honors include the Tokyo International Great Quilt Festival, International Quilt Week Yokohama, and the International Quilt Festival in Houston where *Alice's Kitchen* was awarded first place in the whimsical art quilt category in 2013 by the International Quilt Association.

Alice's Kitchen is part of a trilogy she began in 2009. The other two quilts in the series are titled *Challenge* and *Labyrinth*. *Labyrinth* was awarded a prestigious judge's award by Jacqueline M. Atkins, Ph.D., at the 2009 Tokyo International Great Quilt Festival.

Each of these large, creative works incorporates bold, graphic elements with an incredible array of colors that somehow blend perfectly. The quilts are expertly pieced and machine quilted. There is no paint on the surfaces and all her fabrics are purchased commercially or from specialists who sell hand-dyed fabrics.

While each quilt has its own curiosities, there are common elements to each design in the trilogy. For example, each quilt includes an image of a door. These doors are meant to represent the pathway to the artist's past, present, or future.

Alice's Kitchen is an imaginative recreation of a kitchen from *Alice in Wonderland*, assuming there had been a kitchen. The unconventional objects placed around the room immediately draw the viewer in. The quilt also holds a visual surprise. Sitting atop the table in the center of the room is a kitchen scale with a pointer and two dots that resemble a face. As the viewer moves from side to side, it appears as if you see the face and the face sees you. In other words, the depth of field for the center of the image changes slightly when viewed from different angles and as a result, the face seems to move.

Miki relied on traditional Japanese art history techniques to create these visual surprises, including techniques from *byōbu*, which are paintings done on a folding screen, and *tenjouga*, which refers to art traditionally painted on temple ceilings. She chose to reference a famous Japanese painting known as the "Cloud Dragon" which is painted on the ceiling of a temple in Kyoto. No matter where you move inside this temple, the dragon's eyes appear to follow you.

Challenge is another large quilt with a visual surprise. In this one, the words *challenge, chance, change, courage,* and *Chizuru* are spelled out, but they are done so in the most subtle

Contemporary quiltmaker Miki Murakami has been honored in international competitions for her colorful and sometimes whimsical works of art.

Miki Murakami. *Alice's Kitchen*, 2011. Cotton, organza, felt, wool, imitation fur, and other fabrics: 75 × 91 in. (191 × 233 cm). Hand appliquéd, machine pieced, machine quilted.

For this imaginative quilt, Miki Murakami created a pretend kitchen that would fit easily in the make-believe world of *Alice in Wonderland*. The quilt was awarded first place in the whimsical art quilt category at the International Quilt Festival in Houston in 2013. This expertly pieced art quilt includes a huge visual surprise—the "face" of the scale on the kitchen table follows the viewer's eyes from side to side.

Miki Murakami. *Labyrinth*, 2009. Cotton, hand-dyed satin: 94 × 90 in. (240 × 228 cm). Hand appliquéd, embroidered, machine pieced and quilted.

This quilt is part of a trilogy (with *Alice's Kitchen* and *Challenge*) created by Miki that explores the many choices we face in a lifetime and includes abstract imagery depicting both the unknown and the future. On each quilt in the trilogy there is at least one door, meant to represent the decisions we face in our passage through life. *Labyrinth* was awarded the prestigious judge's award from Jacqueline M. Atkins, PhD, at the 2009 Tokyo International Great Quilt Festival.

Miki Murakami. *Challenge*, 2014. Cotton, hand-dyed fabrics, custom buttons: 87 × 80 in. (221 × 204 cm). Hand appliquéd, embroidered, machine pieced and quilted.

Challenge is a work of art that showcases Miki's talent as an artist. In particular, this works shows a masterful use of perspective, color, and design for maximum impact. At first glance, one sees an abstract design and swirls of line leading to a world beyond. On closer inspection, letters, and eventually entire words, emerge. The letters in this quilt spell several words: *challenge, chance, change, courage* and *Chizuru* (the name of Miki's mother).

of ways and at first glance they are hardly noticeable. Chizuru was the name of Miki's mother and Miki recalls that her mother always challenged her to see the world in new ways, so she made this quilt as a challenge to herself and also to honor the memory of her mother.

Miki is at the forefront of a new generation of brilliant Japanese quilters who are creating distinct original designs and have no qualms about integrating their work into the international quilt scene.

Makiko Aoki had been quilting by hand for 20 years when she happened to see a demonstration by Noriko Endo at a quilt event. She was fascinated by the non-traditional approach to making a quilt top and also by the use of a machine to do free motion quilting. She eventually began taking classes from Noriko and has since perfected her own original designs using techniques that are inspired by her teacher.

Her quilt *Cherry Blossoms at Night* was accepted into the original design category at the Tokyo International Great Quilt Festival in 2014. She drew upon the popular Japanese cherry blossom to create this beautiful landscape, and she chose to set the scene at night when the moonlight shimmers perfectly on the falling petals.

MAKIKO AOKI: A QUILT LESSON THAT CHANGED HER ART

Makiko Aoki. *Cherry Blossoms at Night*, 2013. Cotton, tulle: 46 × 67 in. (116 × 170 cm).

This quilted landscape features cherry blossoms lit up by the moonlight. Makiko has been quilting for twenty years and she has recently expanded her skills to create original designs. This intricate artwork is made using tiny pieces of fabric that have been cut up and carefully scattered in a precise way to form the entire image, a technique she learned while studying under her teacher, Noriko Endo.

ARTISTS SUPPORTING ARTISTS: JIM HAY AND MIKIKO TAKASE

Even farther outside the box of the formal system are contemporary artists who are gathering in studios in Japan in much more informal settings to encourage each other and learn from each other.

Jim Hay, an American-born artist who has spent much of his adult life in Tokyo, and his "student" Mikiko Takase are an example of this arrangement.

Jim came to Japan in the 1990s for a two-week visit as part of a trade delegation from Battle Creek, Michigan. During this trip, he was invited to come back and teach an art class. He readily accepted the invitation and after that return, he simply never left Japan. His first art was sculpture and painting, but he eventually found his way to textiles and began quilting in the late 2000s.

Mikiko Takase, or Mickey as she is known to friends, is a quilter who learned to quilt at Tokyo's formative quilt school, Hearts & Hands Patchwork Quilt School. This instruction followed the *iemoto* traditions and Mickey is certified as an instructor. She currently teaches a group of dedicated students in traditional quiltmaking similarly to the way she learned, but she is also a student herself who is exploring completely new methods, including machine quilting and improvisational techniques. In this way, she represents an emerging group of contemporary quilters who are exploring the wide world of modern art quilt practices.

CENTER LEFT
Mikiko Takase. *Fairy Circle*, 2011. Cotton: 98 × 98 in. (250 × 250 cm). Appliquéd, embroidered, hand quilted.

This dramatic hand appliquéd quilt was created using traditional Hawaiian techniques where the design is cut all at once from one piece of fabric, similar to the way children would fold a sheet of paper and cut out shapes to make a snowflake. This quilt was featured at the Tokyo International Great Quilt Festival.

His quilting and sewing machine skills are completely self-taught. For Jim, using the sewing machine's foot pedal to speed up and slow down reminds him of the gas pedal on the car and this idea encourages him to "race around the cloth" while stitching in free motion.

His student Micky, as she is known to her friends, was originally a product of the *iemoto* system. She studied quilting formally with the Hearts & Hands Patchwork Quilt School beginning in 1982. Micky progressed through the school and received the coveted "instructor" certification in 1990.

She is now an instructor herself for a fairly large group of quilters. Although her curriculum is not as strict as other schools', she focuses the quilt classes that she teaches on traditional techniques and hand quilting.

Interestingly, when it comes to creating her own quilts, in 2008 she began a journey to step completely outside her comfort zone. She is now a student herself who is exploring an alternate world to the ones in which she grew up and currently teaches.

After studying with Jim Hay, she is learning to set aside traditional sewing methods, as well as the traditional tidy treatment of thread and seams, and she is learning to think about applying fabric to a quilt top and piecing it together in ways she never imagined before. Her contemporary quilts today are a hybrid of machine quilting and handwork.

In this way, she is just one example of a new trend of emerging artists who are machine quilting for the first time and learning that dangling threads are not necessarily a mistake, but can be an effect, and that improvisational placement of fabric is okay, perhaps even desirable.

Jim Hay, *Sad Eyes*, 2011. Cotton and other fabrics: 28 × 92 in. (71 × 233 cm). Raw edge appliquéd, machine quilted.

This quilt is a self-portrait by Jim Hay. Jim is an American artist who has spent most of his adult life in Japan.

Mariko Akizuki. *Crossroads*, 2004. Inkjet printed fabric, *Oshima-tsumugi* silk: 76 × 76 in. (194 × 194 cm). Hand pieced, hand appliquéd, machine quilted.

Mariko chose the theme of crossroads to visually depict how the beauty of the past coexists with modern Japan. The quilt itself is also a crossroads of sorts. The images are created using modern computer printing and then they are intersected with *Oshima-tsumugi* silk blocks. This silk is created using the same methods that have been used for a thousand years whereby the silk fibers are hand-spun, then hand-dyed in a painstakingly long process before the cloth is woven. In addition to these old and new textiles, the techniques used to complete the quilt are also a hybrid in that it is pieced using traditional handwork, but it is quilted using a modern machine.

BOTTOM RIGHT
Quilt enthusiasts enjoy attending live demonstrations, workshops, and lectures by award-winning quilters to learn their techniques and improve their own skills. In this photo, Yoshiko Kurihara demonstrates how she made *Masquerade*, a quilt which was awarded the Grand Prix at the 2006 Tokyo International Great Quilt Festival. It was machine pieced and machine quilted.

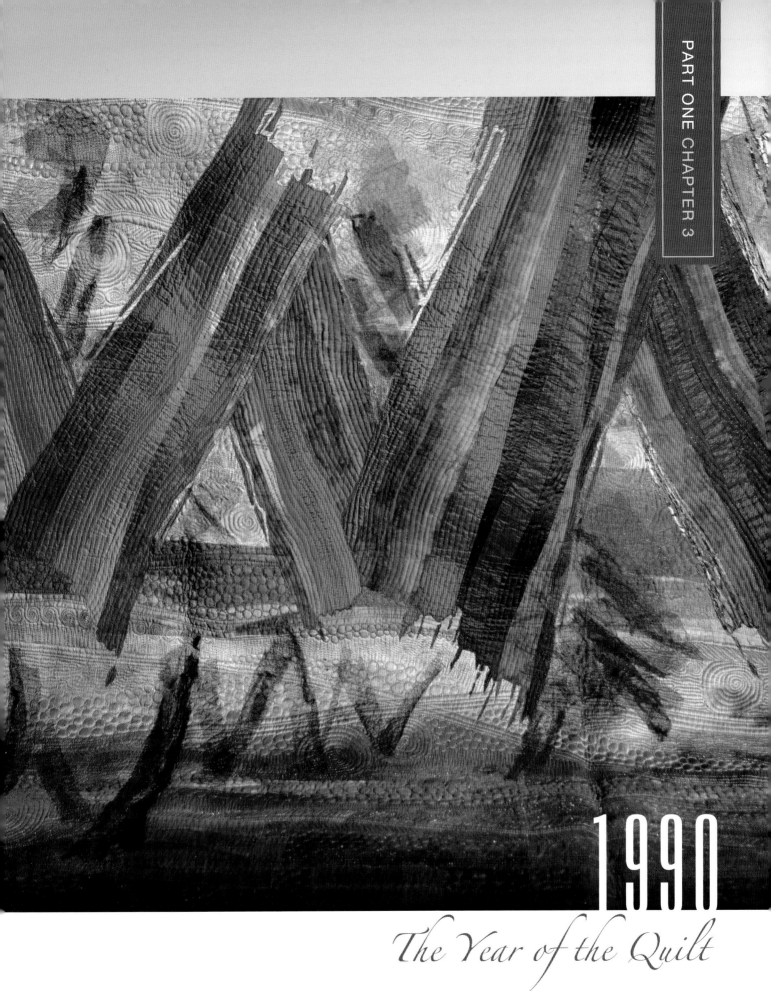

1990

The Year of the Quilt

Finally, after several decades of exploration and adaptation, the stars aligned and by almost any measure, 1990 became the year of the quilt.

For starters, to set the stage one of the first seminal books featuring the work of contemporary Japanese quilters as artists was published in English (1988).

Second, the Japan Handicraft Instructors Association (JHIA) launched their very first juried quilt competition, the Quilt Nihon.

Third, an enterprising curator collected the best quilts of her generation and convinced an American quilt museum to exhibit these, fulfilling her tireless effort to gain international exposure for Japanese quilts.

Fourth, the International Quilt Festival in Houston, Texas, chose 1990 and the sixteenth anniversary of the Festival to mark as "The Year of Japan."

Fifth, 1990 is regarded as the beginning of a two-way international exchange whereby quilt instructors, designers, and curators from Japan traveled to the West and American and European quilt professionals traveled to Japan on a regular basis. In both directions, these individuals brought a fresh perspective and contemporary ideas to audiences eager to learn.

Jinny Beyer, Kaffe Fassett, Libby Lehman, Roberta Horton, and Michael James were among this first group of recognized quilters and business owners who shared their time and talents with Japanese quilters during the decade.

Kumiko Sudo and Emiko Toda Loeb were the first Japanese instructors to begin teaching classes at the International Quilt Festival in Houston, where quilters from around the world were keen to learn their techniques. Many others followed in their footsteps.

Noriko Endo. *Forest in New England*, 1996. Cotton, tulle: 84 × 55 in. (210 × 135 cm). Machine appliquéd and quilted.

This quilt was one of the earliest large, nature landscape quilts Noriko Endo made using her unique confetti method whereby tiny pieces of fabric are carefully sprinkled onto the quilt top. She began exploring this method in the early 1990s and since then, her technique has become a recognized style that is emulated by quilters all over the world.

Japan's first art quilt book written in English, titled simply *Japanese Quilts*, was published in 1988. The authors Jill Liddell and Yuko Watanabe describe how quilters originally adopted American patterns and assimilated them by adding Japanese imagery and using purely Japanese fabrics, such as silk kimono and indigo cotton.

Hundreds of images are included, and the quilts are shown in the book much the way paintings would be shown in a traditional art book. The publication of *Japanese Quilts* marked a notable turning point in Japan's quilt history because it was the first art book to bring contemporary Japanese quilts to an English-speaking audience.

PUBLISHING FOR AN INTERNATIONAL AUDIENCE

KEIKO GOKE'S INDIGO/LOVE/ME

Keiko Goke. *Heart II*, 1993. Cotton: 60 × 68 in. (152 cm × 172 cm). Machine pieced, hand embroidered, hand quilted.

The brightly colored quilts made by Keiko Goke are a constant presence in the story of Japan's quilting history. This one was made in 1993, just a few years after Keiko and other artists were featured in the pivotal *Made in Japan: American Influence on Japanese Quilts* exhibition shown in the U.S. in 1990.

When Keiko discovered this beautiful fabric, she readily went to work preserving it and giving it new life. By reclaiming it, she exemplifies the deep affection the Japanese people feel for their own textiles.

With this particular quilt, some of the pieces were so old and threadbare that the quilt required extra stitching just to hold it together. At the same time, the fabrics were a clear representation of the Japaneseness that was emerging in quilt making at the time.

What is most exciting about this particular quilt is its contemporary design. It is neither American nor traditional Japanese, rather it is a fresh adaption of bold and modern geometric shapes rendered in a seemingly random scheme. This quilt is radically different from an ordinary, or patchwork, quilt and this early recognition in the Liddell/Watanabe book of Keiko Goke's unique vision and talent helped solidify her career as an internationally recognized quilt maker and artist.

KEIKO GOKE is a gifted quilter who has been perfecting her art for 40 years. She is one of the artists featured in the Liddell/Watanabe book and has shared her story in this book as well.

Keiko's 1985 quilt, which is incorrectly labeled *Monpe Quilt* in the 1988 book, is actually titled *Indigo/Love/Me* and features vintage Japanese indigo-dyed cottons, silk, and solid cottons. The vast majority of the fabrics in this historic quilt were given to Keiko by the daughter of one of Japan's National Living Treasures. Her name was Ayano Chiba and she was a one-woman industry who grew her own indigo plants, harvested them, weaved her own textiles, and then hand-dyed them in traditional Japanese indigo. Her textiles are widely respected across Japan.

QUILT NIHON IS BORN

JHIA, buoyed by the success of their quilt instruction program and the tremendous success of the 1988 *World Quilt Festival* they coproduced in Tokyo with the newspaper *Asahi Shimbun*, wanted to create a competition to feature the best of Japanese quilts alongside entries they hoped to eventually attract from other countries.

The call for entries for the first Quilt Nihon (*Nihon* is the name for Japan) competition went out in 1989 and the winning quilts went on view in 1990.

The competition's call for entries was placed in quilt publications in Taiwan, Europe, the UK, the US, and Australia. The goal from the very beginning was twofold. First, the organizers hoped to attract international competition to make the event more relevant in the global quilt world. Second, JHIA wanted to provide an opportunity to showcase the quality of Japanese quilts by creating an opportunity for them compete alongside international contributors.

There were 744 entries for Japan's very first Quilt Nihon. When the panel of judges (including American Michael James) gathered to choose a winner for this important competition, they had a wide assortment of quality and creativity to choose from. The judges selected a very "Japanese" quilt by Yoshiko Katagiri titled *Kabuki* as the grand prize winner.

Keiko Goke was honored with the bronze award. Ikuko Fujishiro and Yasuko Saito were also included in this first exhibition.

When the second Quilt Nihon took place in 1991, Keiko Goke was awarded the gold award. All four of these talented and experienced artists are featured throughout this book.

The first of the first, so to speak, will always hold a special place in the collective memory of a program such as this one. In retrospect, Quilt Nihon's first winning quilt, *Kabuki* by Yoshiko Katagiri, seems an apt choice because of its beauty and its Japanese iconography.

The quilt is an expression of her love of theater and Japanese culture, but it is also a masterful combination of stitching, appliqué, fabric choice, and motif created on her trademark black cotton top. As a child Yoshiko often attended traditional Kabuki theater with her parents and she quickly fell in love with the costumes and the scenery. The makeup the male actors wear, the masks, and the larger-than-life costumes made a bigger impression on her at the time than the actual drama playing out on stage.

Prior to Quilt Nihon, Yoshiko had never considered her art anything more than a hobby. But her students, friends, and colleagues from her first quilt school encouraged her to enter the competition, and she explains with complete sincerity that she never expected to win.

The choice of *Kabuki* was a critical decision for the Quilt Nihon judges, because it set the stage for a world-class competition that reflected both Japanese culture and impeccable craftsmanship and quality to the international art community.

Yoshiko Katagiri. 傾-*Kabuki* (detail). 1989. Cotton, silk antique kimono: 79 × 79 in. (200 × 200 cm). Hand appliquéd, hand quilted.

傾-*Kabuki* was awarded first place in the first international Quilt Nihon competition in 1990.

Quilt Nihon is held every other year and is widely recognized as an important competition on the international quilt circuit. There are two distinct categories, traditional and contemporary.

A selection of winning quilts from both traditional and contemporary categories are displayed at the Tokyo Metropolitan Museum first, then the exhibition travels to other Japanese cities and to venues around the world. Several quilt museums in the US often exhibit winning quilts, including the New England Quilt Museum in Lowell, Massachusetts; the National Quilt Museum in Paducah, Kentucky; and in some years, the International Quilt Festival in Houston, Texas, and the International Quilt Study Center and Museum in Lincoln, Nebraska.

In the 1980s, Kei Kobayashi began studying American culture and publishing books, articles, and documentaries on a variety of topics for Japanese consumption. She proudly points to a 1982 letter from a professor at Harvard University who encouraged her to pursue these cross-cultural exchanges and share her findings. After several years of American studies research, Kei found her way to quilts and began devoting herself to a myriad of projects aimed at expanding Japan's knowledge of quilts and quilting, including producing television documentaries, publishing books and magazines, and curating exhibitions. One of her first curatorial projects involved the coordination of bringing 40 American quilts from the Shelburne Museum in Vermont to Japan, for exhibitions in Yokohama and Kyoto.

AN AMERICAN MUSEUM HOSTS THE FIRST ALL-JAPANESE QUILT SHOW

The enthusiasm generated by this highly successful endeavor inspired her to create a similar opportunity to export an exhibition of contemporary Japanese quilts to be seen in America.

So, in 1989, Kei set her sights on the newly established New England Quilt Museum (NEQM). She read a newspaper article about the women who were creating this new museum from scratch and she found the whole idea of creating a brand new museum to honor quilts so typical of American ingenuity. Kei aspired to be a part of this endeavor by bringing a part of her world to New England. Staff of the museum today still recall her unbridled enthusiasm, and her crystal clear vision to showcase the work of Japanese quilters.

At the time, she told the museum staff that if they would agree to host her exhibition, she would secure the sponsors, coordinate curating the quilts, and would arrange for shipment to America. Marie Geary, who was involved with this exhibition at the time, fondly recalls that Kei made good on all her promises.

As guest curator, Kei worked with the NEQM to settle on the apt exhibition title: *Made in Japan: American Influence on Japanese Quilts*. The exhibition ran from July to September 1990, and it is believed to be the first curated show in an American museum to focus exclusively on newly-created Japanese quilts.

Made in Japan also remains one of the most pivotal exhibitions in the museum's history. The museum printed a thin catalog to accompany the exhibition and each quilt is pictured in the catalog along with information about the maker, similar to the way an exhibition of paintings would be featured.

As this show made its way through several American cities, the originality of the exhibition generated a fair amount of attention from the community and media coverage from the *Boston Globe* and the *New York Times*, as well as other newspapers and magazines. These articles refer to the original American influence on these quilts, but also explain how each quilter has made something that is uniquely Japanese.

Yoshiko Katagiri. 躍–*Wodoru*, 2008. Cotton, silk antique kimono: 3 panels, 34 × 55 in. each (87 × 140 cm each). Hand appliquéd, hand quilted.

Yoshiko Katagiri. 躍–*Wodoru* (detail). 2008.

HOUSTON'S SIXTEENTH ANNUAL INTERNATIONAL QUILT FESTIVAL SHOWCASES JAPAN

When Karey Bresenhan and Nancy O'Bryant Puentes founded the International Quilt Festival in Houston, Texas, in 1974, these fifth-generation quilters and native Texans helped place Houston as "quilt central" in the Western world.

True to its namesake, the Festival is designed to showcase international artists, and for the sixteenth annual event in 1990, the founders chose to highlight the extraordinary work of Japanese quilters.

A special exhibition titled *Beauty in Japanese Quilts* was displayed during the event. In addition, hanging from the rafters of the George R. Brown Convention Center was a huge, 40-foot (12-meter) quilt designed by Akio Kawamoto called *Giant Dream Quilt*. Traditional tea ceremonies were demonstrated for audiences during the festival.

It took 1,400 stitchers more than a year to make *Giant Dream Quilt*, which included 35,000 "patches" of material. At the time, it was touted as the largest quilt in the world. It was first exhibited at the World Design Exposition in Nagoya in 1989. Both Karey and Nancy fondly recall the difficulties they encountered in safely hanging such an enormous object from the ceiling of the cavernous convention center.

Long before this showcase event in 1990, however, Houston's International Quilt Festival and its sister event for the quilt industry called Quilt Market both shared a long and influential history with Japanese quilts and quilters.

For example, leaders of Japan's major quilt and handicraft organizations traveled frequently to attend the Festival or Market and in almost every visit to Houston, or another U.S. or European city where Nancy and Karey organized major events, they sought advice and counsel from these two recognized international experts. Over the years, the two generously shared their expertise on a variety of professional topics including world-class event planning instruction, methodology for organizing quilt competitions, and the most successful ways in which to engage the quilt community.

Equally important is the engagement that occurred between these two leaders and the Japanese magazine and newsletter editors and publishers. This special interchange began in the 1980s and continued for many years. As the Japanese media outlets attended the Festival or Market, they received considerable personal attention from Nancy and Karey, and their staffs. As a result, eventually these editors encouraged their readers to enter international competitions, including the competition hosted by the Houston Festival. Karey and Nancy felt strongly that by entering competitions outside Japan, quilters would be exposed to new creative ideas and techniques, and most importantly, they would have venues in which to showcase their exceptional workmanship, and they frequently shared these ideas with the Japanese quilt media.

In the early to mid-1980s, it was rare for the International Quilt Festival to draw entrants from Japan. But by the early 1990s, this dynamic had changed considerably and entrants from Japan were a regular occurrence.

This photo was taken minutes after the opening ceremony for the Tokyo International Great Quilt Festival in 2014. Attendees hurriedly descend the baseball stadium stairs to be among the first to arrive at the show floor. Approximately 230,000 people attend each year to view contemporary and traditional quilts, and to shop; vendors from around the world sell fabric, quilts, tools, sewing machines, and related items.

SHOKO HATANO AND YOSHIKO JINZENJI TWO ARTISTS CAPTURE THE ATTENTION OF THE INTERNATIONAL QUILT WORLD

Shoko Hatano was among the first wave of contemporary Japanese quilters to show her work internationally and to secure a successful international reputation. She made her first quilt in 1982 and she is one of many quilters to explain that she was not inspired by antique American quilts.

In the early 1970s, she and her husband lived in New Jersey and her husband commuted to Manhattan every day for work. They have two daughters, and the youngest was born while they lived in New Jersey. They later moved to California, and eventually moved back home to Japan in the mid-1970s. She explains that when her children were young she didn't have a lot of free time. But as they grew, she began to explore her creative side.

Her first creative hobbies were sewing clothes for her children, as well as making ceramics, wood carving, and knitting. Eventually, her love of fabric led her to begin quilting and she became a student at Hearts & Hands Patchwork Quilt School.

She recalls being approached by Kei Kobayashi in the late 1980s to participate in the *Made in Japan* show. She felt honored and was eager to contribute. However, at the time,

TOP TO BOTTOM
Shoko Hatano. *Color Box #13* (detail). 2010. Cotton, silk: 54 × 79 in. (137 × 200 cm). Machine quilted.

Shoko Hatano. *Tsubaki* (detail). 2011. Cotton, silk: 60 × 78 in. (152 × 198 cm). Machine quilted.

Shoko Hatano is pictured here in her home studio in the Roppongi Hills area of Tokyo. She made her first quilt in the early 1980s and she has dedicated her career to quilting and teaching. Her work has been widely shown in museums in Japan, the US, and Europe. She has authored one book and has been featured in many other books and magazines.

she did not recognize that she was contributing to an important part of Japanese quilting history—a recognition that can often only come with the benefit of hindsight.

After being part of this international museum exhibition, Shoko knew that she wanted to continue making quilts that were innovative. Her desire to be different, and especially the desire to be dramatic, have become hallmarks of her work.

The quilts of Shoko Hatano are impressive primarily because of the sense of drama she achieves through a palette of deep, saturated colors and unusual, sometimes abstract, imagery. Her quilts are also distinguishable by their surface treatment, a technique which she considers proprietary.

Technique and color are equally important to her creative process. She holds a degree in fine art and considers herself a specialist in color. Clearly, this foundation has provided a particular affinity for how to select color and how to apply it.

Besides color, she often infuses her quilts with images of animals. She loves the challenge of bringing animals to life and she would rather do this than focus on intricate details of nature or flowers. The animal figures she creates are always powerful, sometimes wild, creatures… not docile domestic animals laying in the sun.

One quilt features a group of zebras, all crafted from original patterns and drawings. Their black and white bodies are appliquéd to a foundation composed of brown and beige pieced strips. In ordinary hands, this combination could be chaotic. But in the hands of this artist, the result is harmonic and compelling.

Another quilt features multiple images of wildlife, including a three-quarter view of a lion as it roars, a beautifully drawn horse as it gallops, and an eagle who has either just landed on a branch or is poised to take off. These beings are created with a Japanese sensibility, especially the painted horse, which

looks like it is drawn in charcoal and is reminiscent of the work of ancient Japanese artisans who painted landscapes and scenery on scrolls of handmade papers.

In early 2000s, Shoko's art evolved from figurative images to express abstract ideas using powerful strokes of color on her textiles. She has named this series of art quilts the "color boxes." While each one is unique, they all share a rich, painterly quality.

Her work has been included in multiple exhibitions and recognized in numerous competitions, including "Best of Color" at World Quilt & Textile Exhibition in 2008 and the "Minister of Education Prize" at the Tenth Quilt Nihon. In 2011, she was awarded the "Hillary M. Fletcher Persistence Pays Award" at Quilt National, an international competition hosted in the US. Quilt National's goal is to recognize quilting as an art form.

Another internationally recognized contemporary quilter is Yoshiko Jinzenji. She began quilting in the early 1970s while living in Canada. She vividly recalls the time she saw her first quilt and was immediately inspired to make

one. Since then, she has been on a journey toward a career as a quilt maker and creative textile artist.

She eventually earned an international reputation as a fiber artist who creates and designs her own fabrics, which are breathtaking in their natural beauty. She is highly skilled in the use of fiber, including bamboo-dyed fabric.

She also makes extremely inventive, even avant-garde, quilts, and she concentrates her art on a focused color palette, which is most often off-white. She is a pioneer among Japanese quilters for her use of contemporary design and textiles.

Yoshiko returned from North America to live in Japan in the 1980s. Today she teaches and lectures globally, and maintains studios in both Kyoto and Bali.

The New England Quilt Museum is fortunate to hold one of her art quilts in their permanent collection, and her work is part of the permanent collections of many other institutions, including the Spencer Museum of Art in Lawrence, Kansas, International Quilt Study Center and Museum in Lincoln, Nebraska, the Museum of Art and Design in New York, and the Victoria and Albert Museum in London.

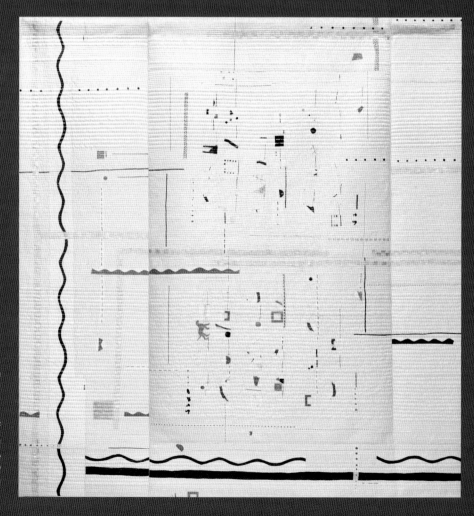

Yoshiko Jinzenji. *Hieroglyphic Quilt II, Mail Quilt,* 2007. Cotton, natural dyed nylon, original design printed cotton: 93 × 98 in. (237 × 248 cm). Machine quilted.

This quilt was made with layers upon layers of translucent white fabrics that were created from original prints custom designed by Yoshiko. A transparent nylon was hand-dyed using bamboo and laid over the entire quilt to provide a warm touch and soft glow.

JAPAN'S GROSS NATIONAL COOL
and the J-Quilt

"WA" QUILTS, REC-OGNIZED FOR THEIR "JAPANESENESS"

In 2002, *Foreign Policy* magazine coined a new phrase: "Japan's Gross National Cool." This clever play on the business term "gross national product" attempts to answer one fascinating question: Just how cool is Japan to the rest of the world?

For an answer, you don't really need foreign policy experts. Ask an average American teenager or young adult to describe the plethora of cultural exports coming from Japan and they could easily point to video games, anime (animated television and movies), manga (sophisticated cartoon novels), Pokémon, Hello Kitty, fashion, even music. Collectively, these innovative products qualify Japan as a cultural superpower and their distinctly non-Western qualities are attractive—some might say cool—to foreigners. In fact, the term J-cool is a very popular label assigned to this phenomenon, as is J-pop, which refers specifically to Japanese pop music.

Some quilters across the globe are similarly attracted to the non-Western qualities of the Japanese quilt aesthetic. They seek the trendy fabrics, unexpected color schemes, unusual patterns, and technical superiority emanating from these quilts—essentially they seek J-cool—even if they do so with little to no awareness of these particular terms or labels. The attraction by non-Japanese quilters to this exquisite aesthetic leads this author to coin a new phrase: the allure of the J-quilt.

But long before J-cool or the J-quilt, the Japanese themselves adopted a charming term to define their own aesthetic. They call it the *wa* factor, or simply *wa*.

Wa is a Japanese word that translates to both "harmony" or "balance," and "Japaneseness." The ancient term is still widely used today to describe art, poetry, music, dance, or other national traditions, including quilts, that contain special qualities that are distinctly Japanese.

Trying to define the *wa* factor, though, is the equivalent of asking someone what it means to be a citizen of their beloved country. Ask a hundred natives and you will get a hundred different answers.

Identifying *wa* within a work of art is fairly obscure, because beauty is in the eye of the beholder, and Japaneseness means different things to different people.

That said, there are some classic, or at least tangible, elements that contribute to a sense of *wa* in quilts.

Most common are the materials, such as the ubiquitous, yet very special, kimono, or traditional indigo-dyed cloth, or even a variety of artisan-made papers. The use of these textiles says to the viewer: "This quilt is part Japanese."

Other *wa* elements can be found in a quilt's subject matter, the environment it portrays, or the style in which it is made.

Japanese people revere nature and are especially attuned to the four seasons. So in many cases a quilt might be considered a *wa* quilt if its subject matter reflects nature or the changing of the seasons, particularly if it has a recognizable element such as a cherry blossom, an image of Mount Fuji, or a rising sun.

The quilts of Noriko Endo, for example, fall into this category. Her nature quilts are recognized internationally for gorgeous landscapes, but they are made all the more special by that very slight essence of *wa*, whether it is a cherry blossom, or the way a blue heron is represented, or how these landscapes depict a love of nature.

When it comes to the work of Yoko Saito, a popular quilter, author, and fabric designer, her sense of *wa* is much harder to pin down, but it most likely stems from her clearly defined taupe color palette. Japanese have a particular affinity for the color taupe because it reminds them of the color of sand, clay, and pottery which has been made from the earth.

Taupe, and the taupe-ism movement it has spawned, encompasses a color palette that includes not just taupe, but also colors such as pearl, sand, many shades of gray, chocolate brown, and even muted green.

Quilters the world over who know the work of Yoko Saito and the work of her many followers, recognize these taupe fabrics and associate them with *wa*, or Japaneseness, even if they do so without knowledge of this term.

Japan's first sign of spring, the beautiful cherry blossoms.

Noriko Endo. *Silk Fiber Elegance, Cherry Blossoms*, 2012. Silk, silk fiber and threads, water-soluble stabilizer: 27 × 56 in. (69 × 142 cm).

This piece of fiber art was created by placing one layer of water-soluble stabilizer underneath and one on top of a fiber art creation; next the layers were machine quilted. When water is applied, the stabilizer disappears and the fibers appear to float in mid-air.

Yukiko Hirano. *Baltimore Album II*, 1995. Cotton: 80 × 80 in. (200 × 200 cm). Hand appliquéd, hand quilted. *Photo by Jim Lincoln. Courtesy of the International Quilt Association.*

Yukiko Hirano was one of many Japanese quilters who created work based on American patterns. This "American Baltimore Album" quilt is part of a series of "Baltimore Albums" she created in her lifetime. Her meticulous hand-sewn appliqué and hand-quilting stitches are representative of the quality of handwork employed by Japanese quilters.

As for her subject matter, Yoko Saito's quilts are closer to American folk art than traditional Japanese imagery. But still, she achieves a very special *wa* factor through her fabric and choice of palette.

WA IN ONE HUNDRED QUILTS

In 2002, and again in 2004, organizers in Japan put together two seminal quilt exhibitions, each featuring 100 quilts.

The collections, One Hundred Japanese Quilts (2002) and Japanese Imagery in One Hundred Quilts (2004), required entrants to incorporate traditional Japanese dyed or woven textiles into their quilts. For the second collection in 2004, roughly 75 of the quilts were made by Japanese artists and for the rest, the organizers sought quilts created by artists of other nations. Quilters were asked to incorporate Japanese beauty, or aesthetics, into their subject matter. As a result, the organizers sought and guaranteed a sense of *wa* in both exhibitions.

These two important exhibitions featured the work of both established and emerging Japanese quilters. This fact made the exhibitions special, perhaps even groundbreaking, because in Japanese culture, the student and master rarely share the same platform.

Yet, regardless of the maker, the primary intent was to show the world that Japanese quiltmaking had matured into fine art.

Jacqueline M. Atkins, PhD., was invited to contribute the introductory essay for the 2004 exhibition catalog. Jacqueline is an American author, textile expert, and academic. She is also well-versed in the world of Japanese quilts, and has made many trips to Japan to judge competitions, curate exhibitions, and lecture at quilt events.

CUTTING UP VINTAGE KIMONOS FOR QUILTS

To some observers in the Western world, the practice of cutting up rare or antique kimonos might seem worrisome, possibly even sacrilegious. But Japanese people feel the opposite way.

For centuries, kimonos, cottons, and almost every type of clothing were recycled and reused, both as a practical matter and a spiritual one. The Japanese assign a spiritual attachment to textiles and other inanimate objects, and therefore the concept of cutting up cloth and reusing it pays tribute to that spirit.

In fact, the ingenious design of a kimono lends itself to easy disassembly. Kimonos are created in panels that are cut from very long rolls of cloth, which are typically only 14 inches wide. The kimono's series of panels on the front and on the back will all be uniform in width, and therefore they can easily be assembled, or reassembled, by rearranging either the front or back panels.

When these kimonos were worn every day, it was typical to try to make them last as long as possible. So, if a section on the back side wore thin, the kimono could be taken apart and the worn panel would trade places with a panel from the front. In addition, mothers would often take apart their old kimonos and alter them for daughters to wear. Scraps, of course, were saved and reused.

These long panels of uncut fabric, as well as kimono scraps, are attractive to quilters for the vintage quality of the patterns and designs in the fabric, but perhaps more importantly, because antique kimonos are usually 100% silk.

Today, this antique silk is highly coveted and depending on its age and quality, it can be expensive to purchase. Some in the quilt industry cite as partial explanation for the high prices the fact that knowledgeable Western tourists and textile aficionados who originally visited Japan in the early 1970s and 1980s began buying up all the antique kimonos. As a result two things happened. First, as demand rose, so did prices. Second, Japanese themselves began to take note of the fact that these individuals were interested in their old clothing and this inspired some to give more consideration to the history of their own textiles.

Examples of small, antique kimono remnants that can be found for sale in Japan today.

The use of kimonos in modern quilting can been seen throughout Japan, as well as in the West. One of the most outstanding artists working with antique kimono appliqué, however, is Yoshiko Katagiri. She is in fact considered a pioneer in the use of kimono fabric for appliqué because of her early adoption of this textile, and her extraordinary technical skill and artistry. Each one of her very special works of art has some element of appliqué made from cut-up kimono fabric.

Ikuko Fujishiro, another successful contemporary quilter who built an international reputation, was also an early pioneer who incorporated kimono fabrics into her quilts, mostly using pieced techniques. Ikuko dedicated her life to quilting and preserving Japanese textiles. She passed away in 2004 at the age of 57.

She was among the first group of enterprising Japanese quilters to exhibit their work internationally. Ikuko's quilts were included in the 1987 Quilt National competition, hosted in Athens, Ohio, and the first Quilt Nihon competition in 1990. She has also been included in other important exhibitions and collections, including the 2004 collection Japanese Imagery in One Hundred Quilts. Houston's International Quilt Festival also organized a solo exhibition of her quilts a few years after she passed away.

These decorative ribbons were once part of traditional kimono costumes.

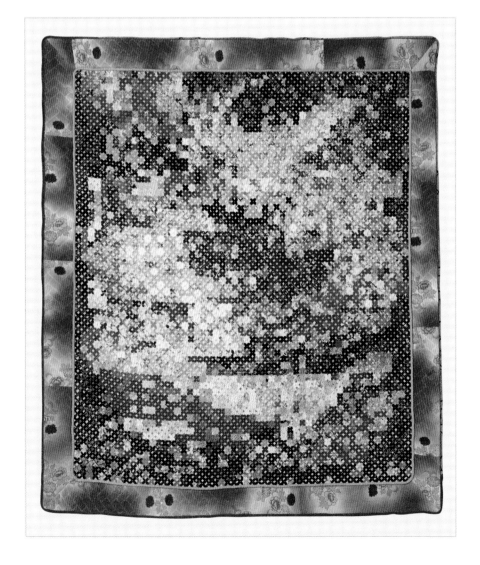

Ikuko Fujishiro. *Cloisonné,* 1996. Antique silk kimono fabric: 75 × 100 in. (190 × 253 cm). *Courtesy of Japan Handicrafts Instructor Association.*

Ikuko Fujishiro was among the first wave of contemporary quilters to incorporate antique kimono textiles into quilts. For this quilt, the artist folded her silk kimono fabric day after day to form tiny blocks which were then pieced together to create this intricate, large quilt. It features an incredible collection of hundreds of tiny blocks made in the style of the traditional "cathedral window" block. Ikuko Fujishiro's art is a testament to her patience and dedication to preserve vintage Japanese textiles in a modern way.

CLOCKWISE FROM TOP

Many temples in and around Tokyo transform into open air markets on Sundays where vendors vie for spots to sell everything from antiques to books to newly made arts and crafts, and even food. Some booths sell a wide variety of vintage textiles and also whole kimonos. Knowing which temple to visit and which vendors to see on which days is an art in itself.

Many residents enjoy visiting the temple markets on Sundays where they can find a huge assortment of antiques and vintage items for sale, including textiles and kimonos.

Stacks of textiles for sale at an open-air market held at a temple in Tokyo.

During her lifetime, she made hundreds of small quilts and approximately 30 large-scale quilts. Often these incorporated thousands of pieces from vintage kimonos that she either inherited from her family or found elsewhere in Japan.

Vintage Japanese kimono fabric is now widely available, both in Japan and at quilt markets and specialty stores in many other countries.

Professional quilters in Japan use various sources to find the highest quality kimono fabric available. In some cases, this might be individual dealers who sell secondhand cut pieces or whole kimonos directly to the quilters themselves, or sellers at the stalls at open-air markets held at various temples and shrines on certain weekends. Knowing which temple to visit on the right weekend and which vendor has the best quality is an art in itself.

However, quilters everywhere, if they so choose, can find small samples of vintage kimono fabric for sale in many specialty quilt stores. In addition, many fabric manufacturers now produce new textiles in cotton, polyester, or even silk, that are exact reproductions of the patterns embroidered, or printed, on older kimono fabrics. This option offers quilters an affordable way to acquire large quantities of fabric and also to achieve a sense of *wa* in a finished quilt.

In this fashion, Japanese kimonos are being preserved by quilters in Japan and elsewhere. The spirit of these old fabrics will live on in works of art, much the same way that some antique quilts in the Western world feature leftover scraps from hand-sewn clothing, or other materials that were recycled into quilts.

Incense is burning outside this Tokyo temple.

Noriko Endo. *Lakeside Solace* (detail of blue heron), 2009. Hand-dyed and painted cotton, polyester, silk, tulle, acrylic paint: 59 × 59 in. (148 × 148 cm). Machine appliquéd, machine embroidered, machine quilted.

Yoshiko Katagiri. 潮−*Ushio* (detail of one fish), 2003. Cotton, silk antique kimono: 79 × 79 in. (200 × 200 cm). Hand appliquéd, hand quilted.

This fish quilt was created using fabric from vintage mens' summer kimonos, called *yukata*. As a result, it exudes a more masculine *wa* factor than is seen on other quilts using women's kimono fabric.

Handmade paper covered in calligraphy. This paper is sturdy enough to cut up and sew into pieced quilts.

PART TWO

EIGHT ARTISTS

Representing Eight Styles of Contemporary Quilting

Now let's turn to a showcase of eight contemporary artists who are currently working in the quilt medium and whose work represents a wide variety of styles and techniques.

These eight artists were selected by the author based on certain criteria.

First, their techniques and artistic output are distinct and recognizable. Among the artists featured here, no two styles are alike.

Second, they have earned a place in the professional quilt world by demonstrating a high level of quality. This quality was proved by having their work exhibited in museum exhibitions, by earning first place honors in major competitions (inside or outside Japan), or via their accomplished teaching careers.

In addition, each quilter has demonstrated over multiple decades a commitment to working with a needle and thread. As a result, their artistic vision has matured with time.

Once those hurdles were met, the selection of artists was narrowed in order to present a variety of artistic styles—figurative, abstract, landscape, storytelling, remarkable pieced quilts, stunning appliqué designs, and taupe quilts.

The artists included here are a representative sampling of the outstanding artistic output of quilting as a contemporary art form in Japan. The stories of how they began, how they have evolved, and how they were influenced by American quilt styles are as diverse as the quilters themselves.

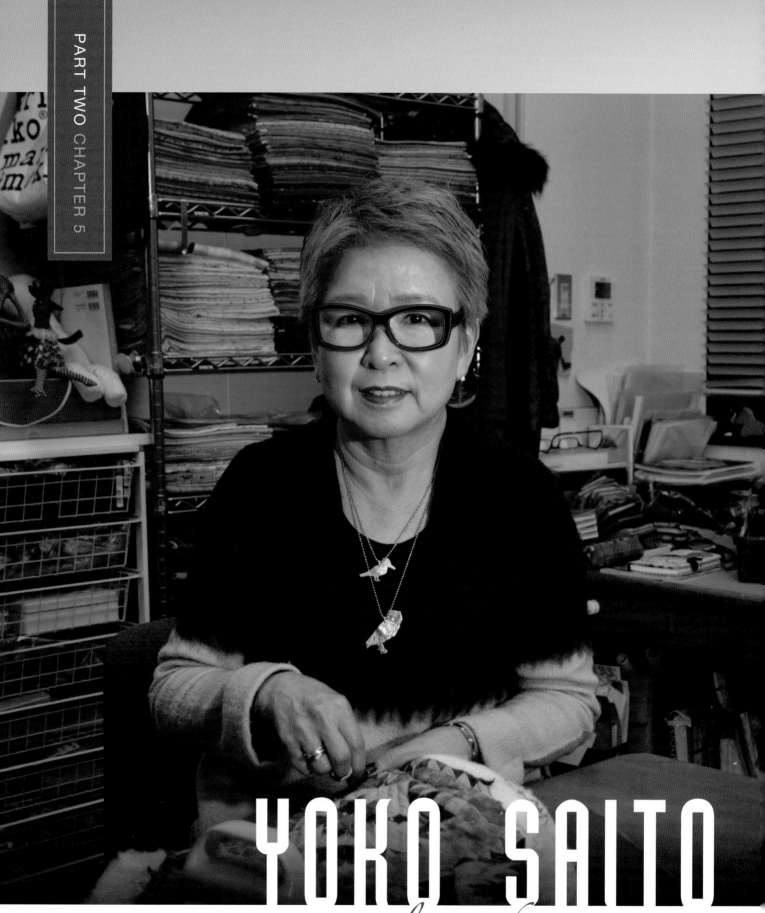

YOKO SAITO

Quilter and Artist First,
Entrepreneur and Executive Second

LEADING AN ENTIRELY NEW MOVEMENT CALLED TAUPE-ISM

Yoko Saito, *Nantucket*, 2009. Cotton: 68 × 73 in.
(173 × 185 cm). Hand embroidered, hand appliquéd,
hand quilted. *Photo by Toshikatsu Watanabe.*

When quilters in the Western world think of Japanese quilters, for some the first name that generally comes to mind is Yoko Saito.

This quiet, successful quilter and business owner is one of the biggest rock stars in the quilt world. And she has an adoring fan base and thriving business to prove the point.

Her rock star status is most evident when she is out and about in Japan, where she is often recognized at stores or restaurants. People often stop her and ask to take a picture or ask for her autograph.

And when she hosts a booth at mega-quilt events in Japan, or anywhere else in the world for that matter, people clamor to get inside her booth and they patiently wait in long lines to meet her and purchase one of her autographed books on quilting, embroidery, or sewing.

THE QUILT PARTY STORY

Yoko Saito is the head of a sewing and quilting global enterprise, Quilt Party Ltd., and she is personally involved in every facet of her business.

She started the company in 1985, and today she and her husband and her staff oversee the production of a line of creative fabrics, write and publish books and patterns, create quilts, purses, kits and other similar items, operate a retail store, supply products to franchised quilt stores, and run a multi-national online business.

Yoko Saito also teaches classes in her store every month and travels often throughout Europe and Asia to teach classes and workshops.

She also is frequently called upon to judge competitions, to speak, or to give lectures to large groups. She willingly accepts the call to judge, but rarely accepts invitations to speak in public because she does not enjoy it.

In Japan, she teaches approximately 400 students. These "students" are actually master quilters who have been studying with her for many years, even decades. A few of her students own and operate independent quilt stores throughout Japan and part of their retail offering includes her fabrics, books, patterns, and kits. In addition, approximately a third of her 400 students also operate quilt schools and provide instruction in her style.

One student received the Grand Prix award at the 2014 Tokyo International Great Quilt Festival for an exquisitely made, hand-quilted taupe quilt made in the Yoko Saito style.

At the center of this enterprise, and the very heart and soul of Yoko's art, is a singular focus on the taupe color palette. Everything she creates stems from her love and mastery of this very special group of colors. She has published taupe color study guides in several languages.

At public events, quilters and sewers line up in long queues in order to have Yoko Saito personally autograph one of her many books. Yoko publishes several books each year and these are treasured by quilters and sewers globally for their patterns and creative use of taupe fabrics. Some of her books are translated. If a particular book is not available in a native language, many sewers buy them anyway in Japanese and study the pictures.

In a rather obscure gray building, located in Ichikawa, an area just outside Tokyo, is the headquarters for Yoko Saito's global quilt business, Quilt Party. Housed in this building are the retail store, classroom, studio, and warehouse to support the online operations. The store features a plethora of taupe fabrics, kits, books, threads, patterns, and related quilt materials.

Yoko began by sewing clothes as a professional dressmaker, and this helped build her technical skills. After she got married, she went to work for a women's magazine that featured a large number of sewing and creative projects each month. Yoko's job was to create those projects, figure out how to communicate the patterns, and actually sew the projects so they could be photographed and featured in the publication.

She placed a lot of pressure on herself to ensure that these products met the highest standards of quality. The deadlines were so tough that she often stayed up all night to finish her work.

She credits these early years, and the pressure to create and produce perfection, with giving her the skills and fortitude to run such a large creative business today.

Eventually she became interested in quilting and had a desire to teach. In 1977, she began receiving instruction from Hearts & Hands Patchwork Quilt School, Japan's first quilt school. It was here that she settled on her taupe palette. She explains that other quilters were focused on bright colors, but for reasons she cannot perfectly explain, she was always drawn to this special hue.

In her published study guide on the theory of Japanese taupe, Yoko defines this palette as encompassing the following colors: blue-gray, charcoal gray, black, beige, pearl, pale pink, orange, dark red cherry, reddish brown, chocolate brown, purple, and light green.

Today, she has made significant contributions to a movement known as "taupe-ism" and the trend is spreading throughout the quilt world.

The Japanese have a special affinity with the color taupe. But this is not what originally drew Yoko to it. Instead, she discovered this color palette by studying American antique quilts.

She recalls seeing the first exhibition of the American antique quilts, now referred to as the Jonathan Holstein Quilt Collection, when they were on view in Tokyo in 1975, and she was very impressed by what she saw.

To this day she feels that her inspiration can be traced to American antique quilts and folk art, and her iconic village scenes and other motifs certainly have the feel of early American folk art.

In her early days of learning to quilt, Yoko collected magazines and books from America and studied what she saw. She made her first trip to the US in 1978 and remembers buying bundles of American cotton quilting fabrics, among other things.

However, when she got home she took out all these bright cotton prints and dyed them using tea bags to mute the colors before she made them into quilts.

She explains with complete and utter sincerity, that she never imagined that her love of taupe would eventually be accepted and sought by quilters all over the world. She pursed it simply because this palette is what appeals to her above all others.

She adds that she has never wavered from this vision. In running and planning her business, which first opened in 1985, she does not conduct sophisticated market studies to evaluate what will sell in one particular part of the world, nor does she spend a lot of time figuring out how to market a specific color or product to quilters. Rather, her business is run from the intuitive, artistic side of her brain.

It is often said that the genius of highly successful retail brands is the ability to anticipate what customers want before they even know what they want. Yoko Saito's brand is a bit like that.

Like many other successful businesses that balance supply and demand, she has discovered something that others want to buy, make, and explore.

When asked how many books she has published in her career, Yoko guesses the number is around 20. Her husband and longtime business partner quickly corrects her and says it is actually 38. By 2014, seven of these have been translated into English, and other translations have been printed in Chinese (for sale in Taiwan) and in French. She has sold many books in Italy, Korea, Australia, New Zealand, and Northern Europe. Quilters in these countries often buy her books in Japanese rather than wait for translations, and the same is sometimes the case for American quilters.

Those 38 books she has authored include only the books published by other companies, and not the dozen or so books that Quilt Party has self-published over the years, which bring

Yoko Saito. *Blue Dragonfly*, 2008. Cotton: 62 × 73 in. (158 × 185 cm). Hand appliquéd, hand quilted. *Photo by Toshikatsu Watanabe.*

the actual number of books in her repertoire closer to 50, as of 2014. The annual Quilt Party photo-book collections feature several quilts by Yoko alongside a wide assortment of quilts contributed by her students, and these books are equally popular among quilters.

In this way, Yoko Saito has come full circle with quilt books bought in a foreign language. The cycle started in the 1980s with her trips to America where she purchased books she could not read, and now today, Americans and other nationalities are buying her books in a language they cannot read. Quilters treasure her books for their photos, patterns, and inspiration, just as Yoko did when she first started collecting books in English—proof that the language of quilting is universal.

A GENRE ALL HER OWN

From the rich colors of the taupe palette, Yoko's quilts are able to exude layers and layers of color and depth. This visual depth is achieved in part by refining the palette to a limited set of colors, allowing the viewer's eye to focus on the extraordinary design and techniques that her quilts offer.

To classify her quilt designs in art terms, they are best described as fitting in a genre somewhere between traditional and modern.

She does not make the typical, repetitive patterns of antique quilts, but her designs are certainly informed by the blocks quilters made long ago. Yet, she finds ways to infuse a modern aesthetic in all of her work, often in unexpected ways. This ability, coupled with her popular taupe-ism, is what sets her apart and places her in the world of contemporary quilts.

Many of her quilts feature long, flowing vines and flowers, and woven or appliquéd vases. Others are collections of blocks spread in an unexpected manner. She's also known for quilts featuring small houses, or whole villages, and these are very much in a naïve, or folk art, style.

Almost all of her quilts feature intricate embroidery stitches, touches that add subtle, yet stunningly complex detail to her work. Her appliqué, embroidery, and quilting are all done by hand.

The vast majority of her quilts are quite large and at first glance, one might assume they are traditional handmade quilts.

But the details start to draw viewers in as they begin to really "see" the quilt: the single vine that stretches and weaves through the entire quilt with no interruptions; the petal upon petal that renders a three-dimensional effect to each flower; the tiny French knot embroidered in exactly the right place to complete the bud; the small bird sitting on the end of a branch; and the woven layers of textiles that form her baskets and borders.

In fact, she loves incorporating woven elements into vases and also using them to form striking, latticework borders all the way around a quilt.

In 2010, she authored the book *Baskets Made from Cloth* which included dozens of photos of real baskets alongside those she made from cloth. The book includes patterns for making baskets, quilted purses that resemble baskets, and the quilt titled *Nantucket*.

Nantucket is produced from just a few taupe fabrics that are used over and over, yet the result is rich in color. The depth of color is achieved by layers of dense appliqué featuring beautiful flowers and stems flowing out of woven baskets on every corner of the quilt. The combination of layer upon layer of appliqué, and the woven baskets and borders of this quilt, make it quite memorable.

Yoko fell in love with these Nantucket baskets, the real ones, during her first trip to Boston many years ago. She actually saw a woman walking down the street carrying a beautiful basket and she chased her down so she could stop her and look at it more closely. However, Yoko does not speak English, so she could not ask the woman where she got it.

But during her stay in Boston, she went to several shops until she located something similar. She recalls with amusement that at the time, she misread the decimal point when converting the dollar price to yen, and as a result she thought these baskets were much more expensive than they actually were. A few years later she visited the island of Nantucket and she finally purchased several baskets for herself.

Yoko Saito. *Merrier and Happier*, 2005. Cotton:
65 × 70 in. (164 × 178 cm). Hand appliquéd, hand
quilted. *Photo by Toshikatsu Watanabe.*

This exploration led her in an entirely new creative direction, and true to her lifelong quest for perfection, she eventually decided to learn to weave these baskets herself.

To do so, she sought out instruction from a teacher in Japan who had studied the method while living in New England. When that instructor realized who Yoko was, she initially declined to give Yoko the lessons because the pressure of teaching such a master instructor was just too intimidating. But Yoko kept asking this instructor to take her on, and eventually, the teacher accepted Yoko as a student.

Living up to the pressure of being such a widely recognized muse of the quilt world, not to mention running a large enterprise, comes with a certain amount of stress of course. Oddly enough, it is basket weaving and other non-sewing creative endeavors that help her to relieve stress and rejuvenate her creative spirit.

But beyond the business, the store, the books, the patterns, the teaching, and the fame, Yoko is a quilt artist first and foremost. She has put in the hours to perfect her craft and because of her talent and dedication, she will certainly continue to be an inspiration to quilters and other stitchers who feverishly pursue her very special world of taupe-ism.

Taupe-ism encompasses a rich palette of multiple colors including blue-gray, charcoal gray, black, beige, pearl, pale pink, orange, dark red cherry, reddish brown, chocolate brown, purple, or light green.

Handmade Raggedy Ann and Andy dolls decorate the Quilt Party store.

Quilt Party sells pre-packaged kits with pre-cut fabrics and instructions to make specific quilts, purses, dolls, and other items. These items are sold online and in this store, as well as at other retail stores operated by the students connected to Yoko Saito and Quilt Party.

For a woman at the head of a multi-national quilting, sewing, and publishing enterprise, the desk of **YOKO SAITO** is surprisingly low tech. No sewing machine. No computer. Not even a smart phone or charger in sight. Instead, there is a plethora of scissors, pens, needles, and other artistic tools. And of course, stacks of neatly folded cuts of her company's branded taupe fabric fill the nearby shelves. They're carefully arranged from light to dark shades. Books and scrapbooks are stacked nearby and she quickly pulls these out to demonstrate the creative process used to prepare her newest fabric designs for production.

She shares this studio space with some of her staff members and her husband, who is an integral partner in her business. Just outside the studio, there is a large warehouse filled with boxes of fabric and related products, and a team of women move about quickly to fulfill online orders from the Quilt Party website. Orders for fabric, patterns, kits, books, and tools are shipped all over Japan and to nearly every corner of the larger quilt world.

The brick and mortar retail store, Quilt Party, is located in Ichikawa, an area on the outskirts of Tokyo. The store occupies one floor, situated below her office and warehouse. At the back of the store is a large classroom. Students sit at closely arranged conference tables so they can take notes. There is a large chalkboard at the front of the room. This is not a studio for sewing machines or other hands-on activities; rather it resembles a common classroom arranged for lectures, a setup familiar to students of the traditional Japanese *iemoto* quilt schools.

YOSHIKO KATAGIRI

Meet the Master of Exquisite Appliqué

QUILTED LAYERS OF FINE ART MIXED WITH VINTAGE
FABRIC AND TRADITIONAL THEMES

Yoshiko Katagiri. 洋−*Ohoumi* (detail), 2005. Cotton,
silk antique kimono: 70 × 70 in. (180 × 180 cm).
Hand appliquéd, hand quilted.

Yoshiko Katagiri lives in the quiet and historic city of Nara, in central Japan. The park at the center of town is a favorite spot for residents and tourists. Deer are revered in Nara's historic parks and hundreds of them roam freely. This town, which was once the capital of Japan, is also home to the world's largest bronze Buddha sculpture.

Living in this ancient city seems somehow appropriate for Yoshiko because most of the 80-plus quilts she has made in her lifetime reflect the Japanese spirit, culture, and love of nature.

Yoshiko has a charming and fun-loving personality that endears her to her friends and family. Part of her happy personality is immediately apparent when looking at her short gray hair, which she dyes in a few tiny sections with spots of blue, just to keep things more interesting.

She is so approachable and engaging that even a stranger will feel like her friend in no time, especially when speaking the language of quilts.

Any description of her work must begin with the fact that Yoshiko Katagiri works entirely by hand. She draws her own images and makes her own patterns, all of her quilts are hand quilted, and she is a master at hand-sewn appliqué.

In fact, she includes appliqué in every quilt she has made and her impeccable needle-turn technique—combined with her fabric of choice, antique kimonos—is a distinguishing hallmark of her work.

She's also made very clear choices about subject matter to create a consistent, and well-respected, body of work. Yoshiko's quilts capture a precise moment in time and reflect that moment back with a distinctly Japanese point of view. They are compelling representations of her past and her culture.

Yoshiko Katagiri. 洋-*Ohoumi* (detail), 2005.

This fierce fighting fish is the epitome of strength, but also exudes beauty through its delicate features. The kimono fabric, the strong colors, and the exquisite appliqué all contribute to give this quilt a very Japanese sensibility.

Yoshiko believes her quilts reflect her *iki*, or her Japanese spirit. She conjures memories of her own childhood, but she also makes art that shares the rich traditional heritage of her country, everything from *Kabuki* theater to *sumo* wrestling, and of course nature and the world around her.

She grew up in Osaka, and she studied drawing in junior high and high school. Sewing was an important part of her childhood and family traditions. One of her favorite items to sew was doll clothes. She had access to plenty of professional inspiration in her family. Her grandmother was a successful seamstress who made kimonos and also taught others her craft.

After she married, she began sewing clothes for her new family. Her two daughters fondly recall the beautiful things she made for them as they were growing up. Eventually, Yoshiko returned to her love of dolls and began creating artistic dolls that she carved and painted, then dressed exquisitely in traditional Japanese costumes. And then she discovered quilting.

Like many quilters of her generation, Yoshiko spent the first seven years of her quilting experience at a traditional Japanese *iemoto* quilt school, first as a student and later as a teacher. These early years of rigorous training within the *iemoto* system instilled the sewing and quilting fundamentals that set the stage for an artist who eventually mastered her craft in order to establish a career as an award-winning quilter and teacher.

Yoshiko Katagiri. 潮−*Ushio* (detail), 2003. Cotton, silk antique kimono: 79 × 79 in. (200 × 200 cm). Hand appliquéd, hand quilted.

Thinking back to her earliest quilt influences, Yoshiko recalls that she was definitely inspired by American antique quilts. When she attended the quilt school, they spent a significant amount of time studying and replicating American quilts and all of the quilts she made during this time were based on traditional American patterns.

Her fabrics were even imported American cottons, and she made her quilts with the help of American tools.

In those early days of learning to quilt, there were very few Japanese books or instruction manuals, so schools acquired information about American culture from books, magazines, even television.

Yoshiko's American influence stems partly from her fond memories of watching episodes of *Little House on the Prairie* on TV. In fact, *Little House on the Prairie* influenced many

AMERICAN INFLUENCE:
ANTIQUE QUILTS AND *LITTLE HOUSE ON THE PRAIRIE*

would-be Japanese quilters by creating a romanticized view of life in America's early pioneer days and instilling strong visual images of beautiful American quilts.

The series about the pioneer days in the American West was based on the novels of Laura Ingalls Wilder. It aired in Japan in the 1970s and 1980s. The scenes where the mother patiently worked on her quilts after the day's chores were done were especially meaningful to Yoshiko.

QUILTING FOR THE LOVE OF FABRIC

Yoshiko has a massive collection of vintage kimono fabric and she's been incorporating parts of her collection into her quilts for nearly 30 years. In this regard she is not alone. There are many Japanese artists who make use of antique, or vintage, kimono fabrics.

But the quality of Yoshiko's appliqué is superb, and perhaps in a class by itself. Her long, sometimes swirling lines of appliqué are so precise, one might think she has used commercial cording or pre-cut templates rather than handcrafting these delicate pieces.

Even upon the closest inspection, her appliqué stitches are nearly invisible. The other defining characteristic of her work is the way she mixes the appliqué image with an image depicted by a quilted line, often with one dependent on the other to complete the idea, or one echoing the other. Friends often refer to this combination as a "Katagiri quilt."

Her subject matter typically consists of fish, insects, flowers, or traditional characters based on her original drawings and patterns.

The foundation for the vast majority of her quilt tops is a specific blend of black cotton, which she has custom dyed to her exact specifications by a dye specialist in Kyoto. This particular black is a few shades lighter than pitch black. She specifically chose this color because it reminds her of the color of *sumi* ink, which is often used in calligraphy. To Western sensibilities, the color might be described as one that is close to the color of an old-fashioned chalkboard, black with a slightly dusty layer of chalk.

Yoshiko Katagiri. 茜–*Akane* (detail of one dragonfly), 2001.

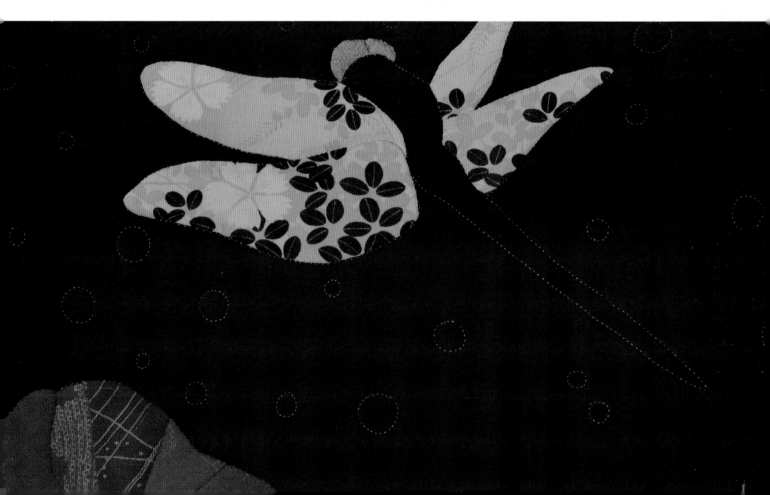

Yoshiko Katagiri. 光–*Corona*, 2006. Cotton, silk
antique kimono: 79 × 79 in. (200 × 200 cm).
Hand appliquéd, hand quilted.

Intense red and yellow flames from the sun dominate this powerful quilt. The yellow is especially
impactful because antique yellow kimonos are rare. Experienced quilters such as Yoshiko have
numerous sources in Japan to find rare and special antique fabric.

Yoshiko Katagiri. 光–*Corona* (detail), 2006.

DRAGONFLIES PLAY THE PART OF SUMO WRESTLERS

Among her growing quilt collection—the vast majority of which she still owns because she can't bring herself to sell her quilts—she does have one favorite which surprisingly deviates from her trademark black foundation. It's titled *Tsuwamono* and was made in 2003.

Tsuwamono is made with vintage fabrics and depicts a classic sumo wrestling scene, using dragonflies instead of human wrestlers. Two large dragonflies are posed exactly as two massive sumo wrestlers would stand as they square off against each other.

It is important to note that the choice of dragonflies to depict wrestlers is not a random choice. In Japanese culture, the dragonfly is associated with martial arts and the various names in Japanese language for this insect are associated with victory.

While growing up, Yoshiko attended many *sumo* matches with her father and she is still a fan of the sport today.

Sumo wrestlers adopt a color for their *mawashi*, or loin cloth. The choice of color is considered very carefully and can be changed depending on the event or competitor they face. Yoshiko's favorite wrestler, Musōyama Masashi, is now retired, but the pumpkin-pie colored background on this quilt top is the color Musōyama wore in one of his biggest victories.

The dark blue-black and gray fabric for the wings of the dragonfly on the right is particularly precious to her because it is from clothing once worn by her father. The top portion of the wing on the right side of each dragonfly is created using reverse appliqué and the fabric is more than 150 years old.

Rather than clutter this quilt with close, complex stitching lines, Yoshiko chose seemingly light and long swirling lines for her hand quilting, which gives the whole quilt a modern feel and helps reflect the motion of two dragonflies.

A second quilt with dragonflies as the central subject depicts smaller versions of the insect flying around and scattered in every direction. Yoshiko chose to make 66 dragonflies on this quilt because that was her age at the time she created it.

Yoshiko Katagiri. 力–*Tsuwamono*, 2003. Cotton, silk antique kimono: 59 × 59 in. (150 × 150 cm). Hand appliquéd, hand quilted.

A pumpkin-pie shade of orange is used for the background of this stunning quilt, a departure from the hand-dyed black quilt foundations Yoshiko uses most often. She chose this unusual color because it is the color associated with a particular victory match from her favorite sumo wrestling star, Musōyama Masashi. The two dragonflies are positioned as human wrestlers would stand to begin a match. This particular insect was chosen because in Japanese culture the dragonfly is often associated with victory in battle.

Each dragonfly is lovingly appliquéd, of course, and every piece of fabric is from kimonos worn by men during the summer season, which gives this particular quilt a bolder, more masculine feel.

In addition to the dragonfly, powerful images of fish are particularly intriguing to Yoshiko. In Japanese writing, the character for the sea is composed of a mother inside herself, and for Yoshiko this idea of the sea and Mother Nature being intertwined is a compelling one that she returns to again and again.

Ohoumi might be one of her strongest quilts based on this idea. It depicts a single, large fish on a black background. His face is fierce and is punctuated with tough spikes emanating from his head and above his mouth. Yet, he has a beautiful, soft blue eye and his body is somehow delicate and shown only as a skeleton. His fins are strong red lines heading up and out to push him through the water. He is surrounded by small dots of white appliquéd silk, echoed by circular quilted lines, appearing as white and black bubbles floating upward through the sea.

Yoshiko returned to image of the fish again for the quilt that she exhibited at the 2014 Tokyo International Great Quilt Festival, in the section showcasing the work of 60 invited artists.

This one, titled 大−*Yuttari* (*Peaceful*) (see page 24), is a giant whale with his tail fin breaking out of the plane of the quilt and jutting into the air. His body is depicted with a series of red appliquéd circles, and again, the circles continue out into the water with the silk appliqué echoed by a circular quilted line. Swimming alongside him is a smaller remora fish, also known as a suckerfish.

There is a visual surprise that cannot be seen by most viewers, and it's on the back. Another whale, a baby one, is appliquéd on the back in a mirror image to the one swimming on the front.

大−*Yuttari* (*Peaceful*) attracted a steady stream of viewers at the Tokyo exhibition and many stopped to study the appliqué and appreciate the strength and creativity of this particular work of art.

Another quilt showing the intense power of nature is a red and yellow image of the flaming sun. Rather than show a docile round ball in the sky, Yoshiko chose to exhibit the sun's full wrath by representing the rays as flames. In fact, at first glance one might think this is an ordinary fire, but in the very bottom of the quilt, there is a solid arc of the sun's surface and the flames emanate from it. These flames fill almost the entire quilt and are made with an incredibly intense color palette of mostly yellow silk kimono fabrics punctuated by splashes of red. The choice of yellow is especially interesting because vintage yellow silk kimonos are rare in Japan.

The beautiful red and yellow fabric combination is blended so perfectly that it seems to actually ooze heat, almost as if one can feel the warmth coming from these swaying flames.

Hunting down all these old kimonos is no simple task. Yoshiko is constantly on the lookout for the perfect fabric and if she finds it, rarely does she pass up a chance to purchase it and bring it home. Then, when she starts working on her quilt, she pulls dozens and dozens of pieces from her collections and searches and searches until she finds the exact piece of silk with the exact color combination she wants. She admits she creates quite a mess in her studio. But Yoshiko is fortunate to have two dutiful daughters nearby to help her clean up.

The whole experience of shopping for fabric, searching her collection for fabric, cutting it up, and finally incorporating it into her art is the thing she treasures most about quiltmaking, and she frankly admits that like a lot of quilters, she'd rather do these things than cook, clean, or even eat.

PREVIOUS PAGES
Yoshiko Katagiri. 茜−*Akane* (detail), 2001. Cotton, silk antique kimono: 75 × 75 in. (192 × 192 cm). Hand appliquéd, hand quilted.

There are 66 dragonflies on this quilt representing Yoshiko's age at the time she created it. The dragonfly is an insect she has featured several times in her art. It is often associated in Japan with the season of summer and can also represent victory in battle, or in martial arts, such as sumo wrestling.

A quarter century has passed since Yoshiko Katagiri was chosen as the first winner of the prestigious Quilt Nihon. That initial, albeit unexpected, success set her on a path as an international exhibitor and teacher. She has gone on to represent Japan in numerous international exhibitions, including One Hundred Japanese Quilts (2002) and Japanese Imagery in One Hundred Quilts (2004) that toured several countries and attracted considerable attention to contemporary Japanese quilts.

Throughout her career, Yoshiko has followed one main goal, and that is to share her love of Japanese culture and spirit in her art. And by that measure, she has certainly succeeded.

INAUGURAL QUILT NIHON WINNER TO A QUILTER FOR ALL TIME

Yoshiko Katagiri. 禅–*Zen* (detail of the rose in the center), 2001. Cotton, silk antique kimono: 83 × 70 in. (212 × 178 cm). Hand appliquéd, hand quilted.

A red rose is created with antique kimono silk that has been appliquéd in layers to create depth in the flower's many petals.

Yoshiko Katagiri. 清-*Syo* (detail), 2005. Cotton, silk
antique kimono: 24 × 24 in. (60 × 60 cm). Hand
appliquéd, hand quilted.

YOSHIKO KATAGIRI lives in the ancient city of Nara and her suburban home allows her a fairly large studio space. The place is filled with fabric, fabric, fabric. There are dozens of large plastic containers filled to the brim with antique kimono fabric. It is not clear to a visitor exactly how these are organized, but one assumes there is some sort of system.

The interesting thing about Yoshiko's studio is that it is very low-tech. There are no fancy sewing machines, no computers. Yoshiko works entirely by hand and her desk is covered with the hand tools of an artist—brushes, pens, charcoal pencils, and bits of paper cut from magazines for inspiration. Original drawings are scattered all over her desk, waiting to be transferred to her impeccable appliqué.

The front wall has large windows to allow plenty of daylight. The storage closet at the back of the room is home to stacks and stacks of quilts—perhaps 80 or more. She does not sell her work because she simply can't bear to part with her quilts. Each quilt is documented and the location of where it sits in the stack is carefully noted.

Like many Japanese rooms, this room can be multi-purpose. There are side tables readily available to roll in and out to serve lunch or tea.

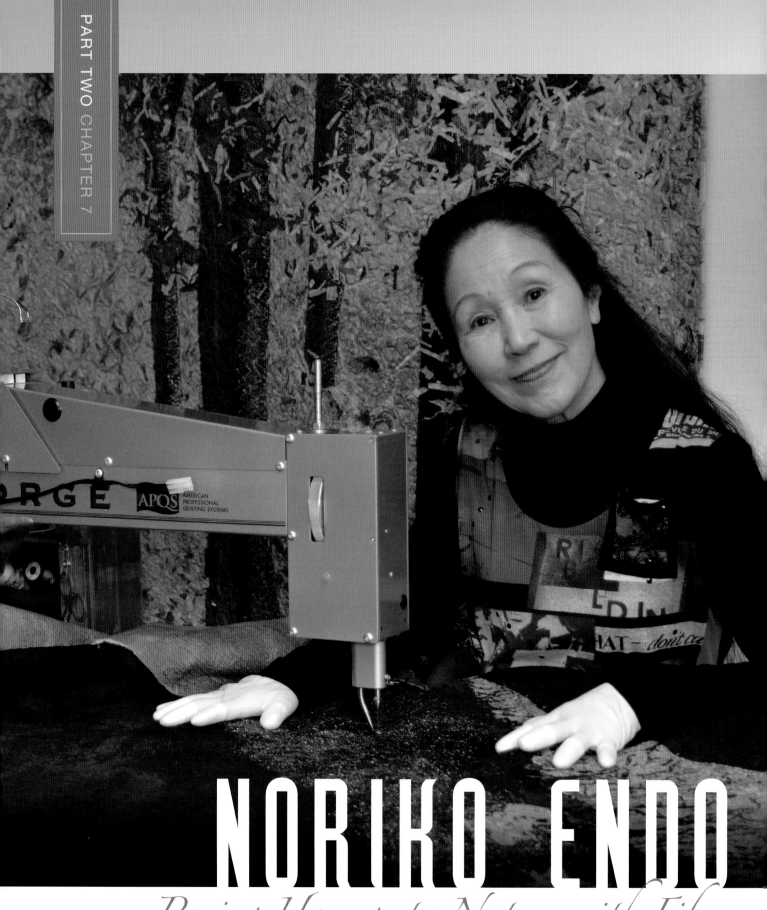

NORIKO ENDO

Paying Homage to Nature with Fiber

RE-INVENTING THE JAPANESE LANDSCAPE

Noriko Endo. *Woodpecker*, 2013. Cotton, polyester threads, paint: 56 × 70 in. (142 × 178 cm). Machine appliquéd, machine pieced, machine embroidered, machine quilted.

After a decade of making quilts with her revolutionary technique using tiny pieces of fabric, Noriko created this nature quilt using a modern, asymmetrical pieced background. The use of paint and unconventional fabrics, plus the vivid colors, contribute to its very contemporary design.

It is difficult to pin down exactly where Noriko Endo lives or works. This industrious woman is constantly on the go, and the term "constantly" is no exaggeration. She splits her days in Japan between two houses and she splits her career among multiple worlds.

She's either alone in her studio creating art, or she's teaching and traveling internationally on a schedule that is hectic by any measure, or she's working as a brand ambassador for one of several notable Japanese brands, or she is out supporting and promoting her students and fellow quilt artists.

Her schedule, her energy, her enthusiasm, her wit, her jet black (never dyed) hair are all enviable. Perhaps it is exactly this frantic pace in her daily life which allows Noriko to so effortlessly channel complete tranquility in her art.

THE QUILTED LANDSCAPE

Noriko is at the forefront of a new generation of artists who are reinterpreting the centuries-old artistic renderings of Japanese landscape to create intricate, modern representations of the natural world.

She describes her art as Impressionist naturescapes, and these large, scenic moments are filled with painterly qualities that draw the viewer in.

Noriko is also emblematic of the many artists working today who are influenced by their native culture, yet have lived all over the world and therefore have a global perspective.

After graduating from college with a degree in English and American literature, she eventually married and in 1977, she put her English skills to work when she and her young family moved to Queens, a borough of New York City, for her husband's work.

No one in their neighborhood spoke Japanese in those days, but she quickly made friends with neighbors, some of whom had also been transplanted from other countries. In later years, the family also lived in Karachi, Pakistan, before returning to Japan.

It wasn't until much later, in 1985, that Noriko made her first quilt. She was inspired to learn after seeing antique American quilts.

Noriko took her interest in antique quilts a step further and began collecting these pieces of Americana because she wanted to hold them in her hand and study them. She found inspiration in their colors, the techniques these quilters used, and the history of these American treasures.

The muted colors of many of the vintage quilts were especially endearing to her because she believed that while it is easy to use bright, flashy colors that draw attention, these quilters were able to communicate emotion through a softer palette. This lesson has stayed with her throughout her art-making career.

It was during a trip to America in 1993 that Noriko devised her trademark technique. One night, her creative invention of making confetti quilts came to her almost all at once, and she set to work immediately on a table inside the home of a friend.

The confetti technique is achieved by essentially chopping up fabric into confetti-sized pieces. Cottons, wool, scraps, vintage silks, kimonos, yarn, almost any fiber will work. The tiny pieces are separated by color and essentially sprinkled on top of a plain whole-cloth foundation—much the same way a painter would apply layers of paint on a white canvas.

She has coined her technique "confetti Naturescapes," and she has written one book under that title in English.

Some of the confetti Naturescape quilts feature the ever-present Japanese cherry blossoms. Originally, each blossom was painstakingly cut by hand and several tiny dots were hand painted in the center to add a touch of realism.

However, based on the popularity of her iconic quilts, she was approached by Accu-Quilt, a major die-cut manufacturer based in North America, and asked to collaborate on a product specifically made to cut several layers of fabric at one time in the shape of a cherry blossom. This has saved hundreds of hours of effort required for one tiny element of her designs.

As for the rest of her quilted landscapes, once the foundation top is prepared and the image looks as it should, a nearly invisible layer of fine tulle is laid over the whole thing and then it is free motion machine quilted to secure the tiny pieces of fabric to the foundation.

She most often uses an invisible thread, or monofilament thread, over the tulle so that the fibers shine through and the quilting stitch fades away. In some cases, though, she will deliberately quilt with a silk thread or other decorative thread for effect.

As it's quilted, some parts are enhanced with very obvious thread embellishment, especially the trees. Her exquisite thread "painting" creates textures and depth, and adds tiny infusions of color and interest across the quilt.

The soft colors and fresh, painterly qualities of the nineteenth-century Impressionist art movement are always in the forefront of her mind when she creates her images. She finds the Impressionist technique very beautiful and she's been inspired by many of the Impressionist and post-Impressionist painters. She's particularly drawn to the brilliant use of color in the flowers and landscapes of Vincent Van Gogh.

However, while her inspiration may be from the nineteenth century, both her technique and choice of subject matter are truly contemporary. To accomplish both is a testament to her artistic maturity: she has the discipline to capture a Japaneseness, or *wa* feel, in her art, while simultaneously making art with a global perspective and universal appeal.

Noriko Endo. *Entering Eden*, 2008.

Noriko Endo. *Entering
Eden* (detail), 2008.
Hand-dyed cotton, tulle:
87 × 74 in. (216 × 185 cm).
Machine appliquéd,
machine embroidered,
machine quilted.

HONORING NATURE

The essence of these dramatic landscapes is strongly grounded in Japan's indigenous love
of nature. Noriko is particularly attuned to the changing seasons and she loves to study nature.
She tries to recapture those special, nearly perfect moments when the light through the trees
is just right.

Her ubiquitous cherry blossoms, her exquisite and beautifully rendered flowers, or the
tender details of a blue heron she watches from her studio window are memorable elements
of her subject matter.

This quilt is one of the many artworks under
construction at any given time in Noriko's studio. She
is constantly experimenting with new techniques,
always pushing herself to expand her skills and bring
new energy and creativity to her quilting.

RIGHT
Noriko Endo. *Entering Eden #2*, 2012. Cotton,
tulle: 86 × 73 in. (218 × 185 cm). Machine
embroidered, machine quilted.

Noriko's quilts have won awards in many competitions, both in Japan and internationally. She was awarded a major prize in the Tenth Annual Quilt Nihon competition, and she has won multiple awards from several years of competition sponsored by the International Quilters Alliance at their International Quilt Festivals in Houston and Chicago. She was the first Japanese quilter to be awarded Best of Show at Quilt National (which is hosted in the US) in 2007, and she has won prestigious awards in many other competitions around the world. She has also been featured in numerous magazine articles and is an active member of the Studio Art Quilt Associates (SAQA). At one time, she served as the SAQA representative for Japan. In addition, she has participated in numerous museum exhibitions and solo shows, including a solo show at the City Quilter's Art Quilt Gallery in New York City. Her quilts have been acquired by collectors all over the world.

Even with these accomplishments, Noriko chooses to continue teaching and enthusiastically gives of her time and talent to her students over and over again. Besides, for her to change her pace from anything but full speed ahead would be the antithesis of her whole spirit.

While many artists are immensely protective of the technique they use to make their art, Noriko freely gives away her method to her students.

As a result, quilters all over the world clamor to take her classes when they are offered at international workshops, festivals, and quilt events. Those lucky enough to live in Japan, Taiwan, and other Asian locales show up at her studio, her home, or one of the other Tokyo locations where she teaches on a regular basis, for encouragement, instruction, and most of all, inspiration.

As a result of this vast influence, one can pick out the "Noriko followers" in quilt exhibitions all over the world. Noriko firmly believes that being able to see these students create mature works of art of their own making that reference her style is the greatest legacy an artist can ever leave.

A TEACHER WHO GIVES GENEROUSLY OF HER TIME AND TALENT

A collection of pre-cut silk cherry blossoms waiting to be incorporated into a quilt.

After creating realistic works that focus simultaneously on the serenity and the drama of the natural world, Noriko is shifting to slightly more interpretative and experimental works of art. She is an artist who has always innovated, yet her new uses of fiber are particularly exciting.

For example, in 2014 she completed a triptych that is vastly different from her Impressionist landscapes. Predominantly black and quilted mostly in black, this particular quilt limits the use of the confetti technique to a single mountain ridge gently sloping across the top third of the panels. She incorporates an ever so slight waterfall using a variety of new techniques: tiny slivers of long fiber, thread, paint, and quilting. The result is a fresh and striking work from an accomplished artisan.

Another side of her exploration ventures into pure fiber art. She has experimented with different ways to assemble a variety of fibers, mixed with her traditional touches such as tiny cherry blossoms. She quilts by creatively stitching the layers together using a technique referred to as thread painting, without the use of the expected batting or layer of backing material. As a result, these stitched fibers seem suspended in mid-air.

Regardless of where her art takes her, one can rest assured that Noriko will continue her passionate drive to teach and produce innovative artistic pieces, and she will zealously continue supporting her students and fellow quilters with the same enthusiasm she has demonstrated over the past 30 years.

EVOLVING AS AN ARTIST

Noriko Endo is exploring ways to use a wide variety of fibers, versus mostly textiles, to express her artistic ideas.

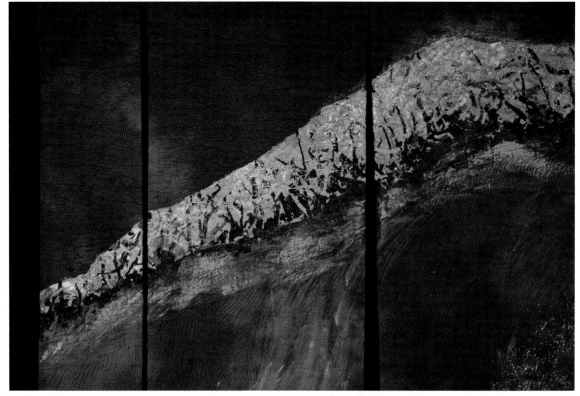

Noriko Endo. *Secret Vantage*, 2012. Cotton, tulle, paint, luminescent fibers: 37 × 25 in. (93 × 63 cm). Machine embroidered, machine quilted.

Noriko Endo. *Sylvan Ambience #10*, 2010. Silk, silk fiber, paint: 15 × 20 in. (38 × 50 cm). Machine embroidered, machine quilted.

Noriko Endo. *Entering Eden #2* (detail). 2012. Cotton, tulle: 86 × 73 in. (218 × 185 cm).

Noriko Endo. *Autumn Splendor,* 2010. Hand-dyed cotton, tulle, luminescent fibers: 72.5 × 49 in. (184 × 123 cm). Machine appliquéd, machine embroidered, machine quilted.

Noriko Endo, *Mother Nature*, 1998. Cotton, tulle, luminescent fibers: 90 × 81 in. (228 × 205 cm). Machine embroidered and embellished, machine quilted.

Noriko Endo. *Guest Appearance #2*, 2013. Cotton, tulle, polyester threads, paint: 15 × 22 in. (38 × 55 cm). Machine embroidered, machine quilted.

Noriko Endo. *Silent Sentinels* (detail), 2004.

Noriko Endo. *Silent Sentinels*, 2004. Hand-dyed cotton, tulle, luminescent fibers: 76 × 66 in. (190 × 165 cm). Hand painted cotton, machine appliquéd, machine embroidered, machine quilted.

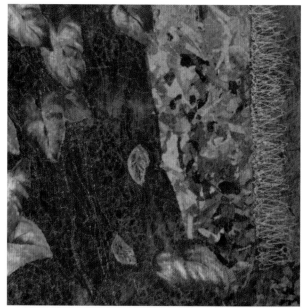

Noriko Endo. *Chased by the Light*, 2006. Cotton, tulle, luminescent fibers: 56 × 44 in. (141 × 110 cm). Machine appliquéd, machine embroidered, machine quilted.

BELOW
Noriko Endo. *Woodpecker* (detail), 2013.

NORIKO ENDO'S primary studio is in her home in the Sengawa district of Tokyo, and it's here where she makes the majority of her quilts. The sewing room is mid-sized and well organized. There are modern quilt-hanging systems on several walls, so quilts can be displayed at varying heights. There is a seemingly endless supply of thread, cones of every color, but there is no visible fabric stash. One assumes it is neatly tucked away, organized by color, ready to be chopped up and used in her unique technique to build the foundation for her quilts. Or, more than likely, there is a supply of silk and other textiles waiting to be dyed to her specific needs at any moment.

Her primary quilting machine is an APQS George (long arm), but there are other machines around: Bernina, Janome, plus a computer, and shelves filled with international books, magazines, and lots of photos. The next room, where her cutting table sits, is a small traditional Japanese-style room with another hanging system. This room has large sliding glass doors to allow plenty of natural light and the floor is covered with *tatami* mats. When Noriko teaches classes at her home, these two rooms are filled wall to wall with students and machines—small tables roll in and out as needed depending on the class size.

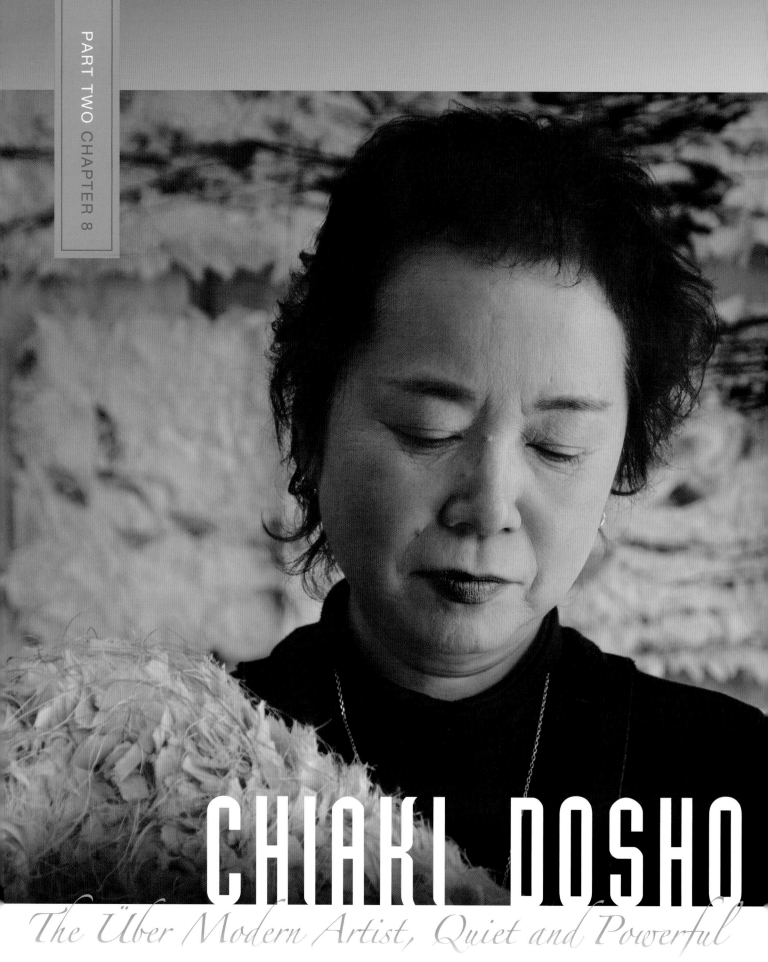

CHIAKI DOSHO

The Über Modern Artist, Quiet and Powerful

THE ETHEREAL QUILTER

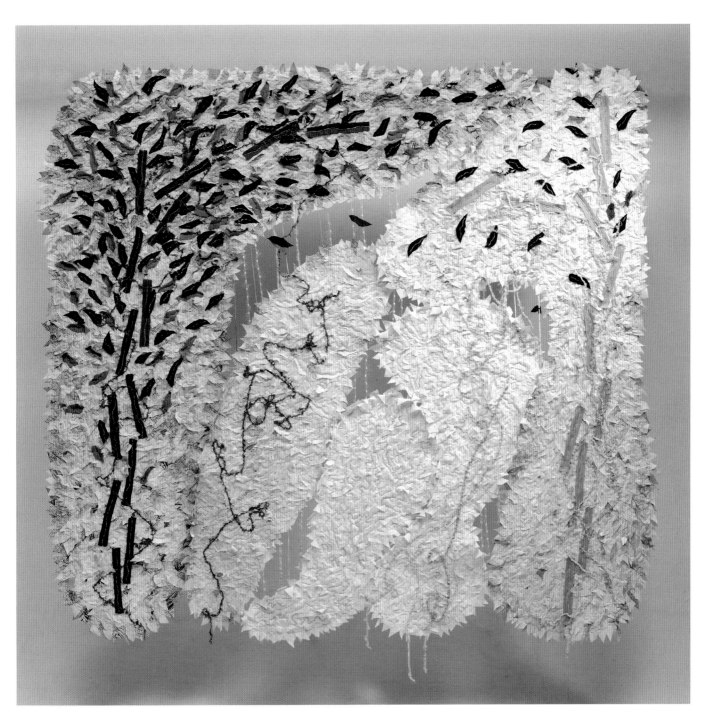

Chiaki Dosho. *Wandering*, 2008. Japanese
antique kimono, silk, polyester, wool: 87 × 79 in.
(220 × 200 cm). Machine appliquéd, machine
quilted. *Photo by Akinori Miyashita.*

This quilt was inspired by a walk in the woods where a distant light captured the artist's
attention and pulled her towards it. Chiaki has recreated that feeling here.

Chiaki Dosho is a quiet artist and her very nature exudes an aura of stillness. From this serenity, Chiaki is able to focus on exactly what she wants and ultimately, she creates works of art that are simultaneously powerful and ethereal.

The surfaces of these exquisite quilts appear to float like feathers, giving them the appearance of fragility, but there are layers and layers of fabric and quilting that also give these textiles a sense of strength.

Because she so effortlessly and beautifully combines traditional quiltmaking with unconventional forms and technique, her quilts can best be described as sitting somewhere between avant-garde art quilt and the fringes of modern art.

STRETCHING TRADITIONAL NOTIONS OF THE QUILT

Chiaki has been making quilts for nearly three decades. Like many of her contemporaries, when she first began she studied traditional techniques at Hearts & Hands Patchwork Quilt School. Eventually, she sought a broader perspective and left the *iemoto* training to pursue a university degree in fine art.

Sometime around the mid-1990s, she discovered machine quilting and free motion sewing and the technology freed her to consider new possibilities. Today, her quilts remain grounded in traditional quiltmaking techniques with the three layers (top, backing, and batting), appliqué, stitching, and so on. Yet she challenges these same traditional techniques and stretches her knowledge to take these stitches and shapes in a new direction.

Many years ago she set out to reimagine the shape of a quilt. No longer satisfied with the traditional notions that the quilt should be a square or a rectangle, Chiaki created her own unconventional shapes. She often strings two or more shapes together with several inches of air in between the quilts. Some of her quilts even have holes, or open-air gaps right in the middle of the form, effects that contribute to their ethereal quality.

To achieve these unconventional forms, she begins by marking a specific shape directly on the batting, and then she cuts it out. Next she prepares the bottom layer of fabric by marking it and cutting it to match the shape of the batting, then the two are stitched together. Now she has a shape and platform on which to begin.

Her next step is to begin the appliqué process. Chiaki's most recent work is made almost entirely with raw-edge appliqué, a technique that many modern quilters employ. Raw edge means that she cuts the fabric and then uses it as is; there is no treatment to the edge and no attempt to hide the raw edge by turning it under.

One distinct characteristic of her technique is that her pieces are not fused to the surface in any way, rather the edges of her cut pieces of fabric float up off the surface and sway if ruffled.

As she stitches her fabric to the surface, she is also testing the limits of the time-honored notion of how threads should be treated. Typically, quilters want very tidy threads with the beginning and end of each stitch neatly tucked away. Chiaki does the opposite. Her quilts are drenched in long, dangling beautiful threads. When viewed from a few steps back, these threads appear to lift up off the surface and float in an entirely new dimension. These threads also add considerable color. For example, in her cherry blossom quilts she often uses heaps of red threads that are left dangling over the all-white appliquéd fabrics.

Chiaki Dosho. *Fluttering Petals*, 2007. Japanese antique kimono, silk, synthetic fibers, wool: 56 × 48 in. (142 × 121 cm). Machine appliquéd, machine quilted. *Photo by Akinori Miyashita.*

Chiaki hand dyes her antique kimono fabrics to create a specific palette. In this quilt, she has scattered wind-blown red cherry blossom petals across a sea of white.

Chiaki Dosho. *Light & Dark II*, 2009. Japanese antique kimono, silk, synthetic fibers, wool: 6 panels, 12 × 47 in. each (30 × 120 cm each). Machine appliquéd, machine quilted. *Photo by Akinori Miyashita.*

This quilt is an expression of the light and the darkness that is associated with life and death, but it is not a straightforward black and white palette. Rather, there are strands of light on the dark surfaces, and vice versa. This is meant to represent the fact that there can be light and hope in death and there are times of darkness in life.

Chiaki Dosho. *The Crossing Times II* (detail), 2009. Japanese antique kimono, silk, synthetic fibers, wool: 78 × 62 in. (200 × 160 cm). Machine appliquéd, machine quilted.

This close-up shows the construction techniques Chiaki uses to connect her unconventional quilt shapes.

MODERN ART, BUT GROUNDED IN A SENSE OF *WA*

Her completely original style and the motifs she pursues help explain part of the mystique of her art quilts. It is this mystique, this ethereal quality, which has attracted the attention of quilters, judges, and art lovers alike.

Chiaki has long been a permanent fixture among contemporary Japanese quilters and her innovative works were included in both of the pivotal exhibitions, One Hundred Japanese Quilts (2002) and Japanese Imagery in One Hundred Quilts (2004). She was recognized in both the 2009 and 2011 Quilt Nihon competitions. She also earned the "Judge's Encouragement" award from Linda Colsh at the 2013 Quilt Nihon.

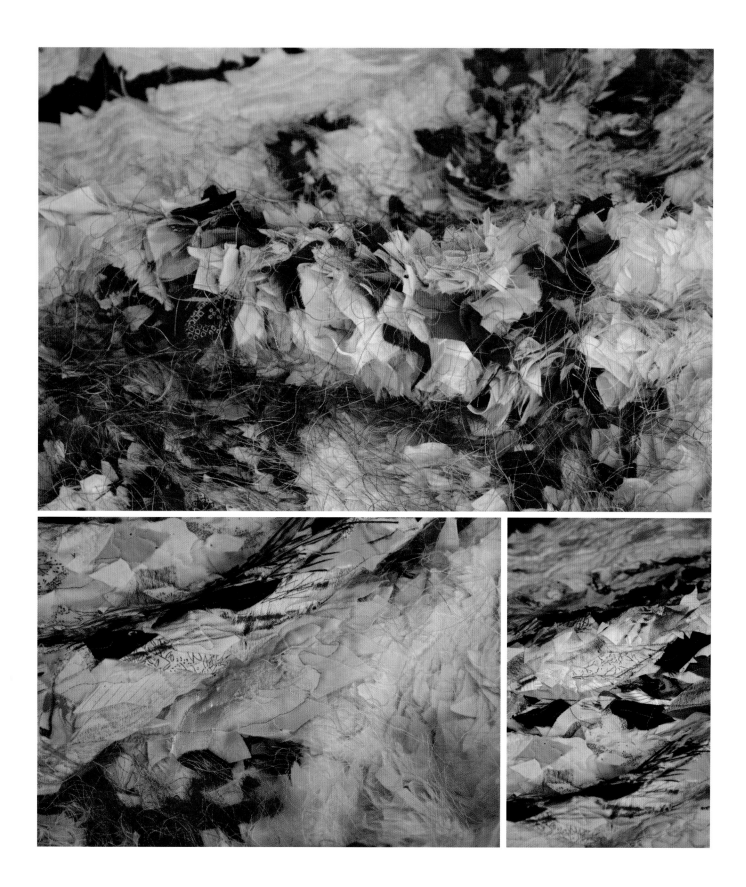

This detail shows how the red and white textiles blend to create an exquisite quilted surface.

Two close-ups show how hand-dyed silk and kimono fabrics are cut and left in their raw form, then appliquéd closely together to create a multi-layered surface for each quilt.

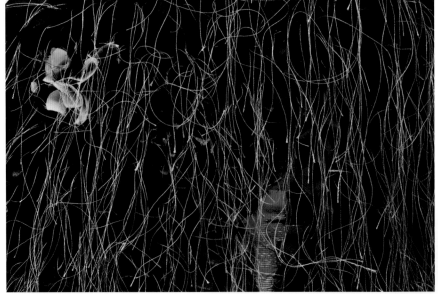

Chiaki has created many innovative sewing techniques that take her quilts to the very edge of modern fiber art. This detail shows how she uses long, dangling threads to enhance the surface design and create an ethereal feeling. *Photo by Akinori Miyashita.*

Chiaki Dosho. *Light & Dark IV* (detail, panels 1–3), 2011. Japanese antique kimono, silk, synthetic fibers, wool: 3 panels, 16 × 35 in. each (40 × 90 cm each). Machine appliquéd, machine quilted. *Photo by Akinori Miyashita.*

She is building an international reputation and her work has been honored in several competitions in Europe. She was invited to display her quilts in France for a special exhibition featuring six artists. Her quilts have also been featured in books, including several collections from the Studio Art Quilt Associates. In 2005, and again in 2007, her work was accepted into the American-hosted competition Quilt National.

Most of her quilts from 2000 onward are variations on a theme. Her cherry blossom series, for example, draws on traditional notions of *wa*, or Japaneseness, with the ubiquitous cherry blossom. But Chiaki takes these traditional notions to a new level by making her pink and red cherry blossoms abstract. These tiny flecks of color are sprinkled across a rich surface of white. This ethereal effect is achieved by a combination of painting with *sumi* ink and the use of hand-dyed textiles. As a result, viewers are reminded of petals floating with the wind.

Chiaki Dosho. *Light & Dark IV* (detail of one panel), 2011. *Photo by Akinori Miyashita*.

For years, Chiaki explored the theme of life and death using primarily black and white. Following the tragic 2011 earthquake and tsunami, she began to express life in blood-red colors for the first time. Neither she nor her family were directly impacted by the earthquake. But Chiaki, and many other Japanese, experienced fear, anxiety and depression about the extreme loss of life and destruction following this disaster. Finding ways to express this grief through art became very important for her.

In fact, to Chiaki the notion of millions of cherry blossoms floating off in the wind each year is the greatest expression of freedom in nature, and it is this freedom to float with the wind that she cherishes most.

Another series she has explored in recent years is light and dark and how we associate these colors with life and death. And here again, rather than take the expected route, Chiaki thinks in uncommon ways. She assigns just as much color to darkness as she does to light, or life. Her black quilts in these series are infused with threads of white, red, even hues of light blue and silver, and she does this because she believes there is hope, peace, even light, amidst the darkness.

The devastating earthquake and tsunami in 2011 hit Chiaki hard, as it did most Japanese. Even though she and her family were not personally affected, she experienced fear, worry, and of course sadness over the immense loss of life. These feelings carried over to her art and she went on to add an entirely new color to her light and dark, life and death series: red.

The red quilts hang in between their light and dark counterparts, and this new color is meant to represent life itself, our heart and soul, but also the loss of blood. And in this new series, large sections of red thread even carry over to both the white and dark quilts to form continuous ideas of how life evolves.

Chiaki's über-modern creations also offer viewers a sense of *wa* because of the fabric that she chooses. The vast majority of her textiles are antique kimonos. She collects these from many sources, including temple markets and other dealers. There is also a family connection that has proved very helpful in the search for kimonos. Chiaki has an aunt who operates a traditional Japanese dance studio, and many of her school's used kimono costumes end up in Chiaki's quilts.

Sourcing old kimonos in this manner works best for her because she cuts so many small pieces that are layered on top of one another, and nestles them so close together, that she requires a great deal of fabric.

Like most Japanese, Chiaki believes she is bringing new life to these discarded, and sometimes dirty or plain or ragged, clothes. Some of her kimonos are extremely old; several are 100 years old or more. She doesn't mind taking in cloth that is marked with stains, holes, or tears because she feels these add to their history and represent the very life they once held. She even goes so far as to take pity on them and loves seeing them come back to life when they are used in entirely new ways in her art.

But unlike most quilters who cherish the colors and patterns of these vintage cloths and use them in ways to accentuate those qualities, Chiaki takes an opposite path. She transforms her kimonos by dyeing them to fit her minimalist color concepts. She also makes use of new fabrics and mixes them alongside her vintage textiles, thus juxtaposing old and new ideas together.

LIMITED PALETTE, INFINITE POSSIBILITIES

Ultimately, each quilt in her contemporary series features a limited color scheme, and in simplistic terms can be described as mostly white, black, or red. Yet, because of her innovative thread placement, fabric choice, floating appliqué, shape, and refined palette—as well as bleaching, painting, and occasionally deconstructing with heat—she achieves something altogether unconventional and free form.

Each quilt is usually infused with the very opposite of its most obvious color: black and red threads dangle on white fabric; tiny pink and red specks float across a sea of white; slivers of white, pink, and light blue are sewn onto the blackest of black.

Somehow, the subtle touches appear both impromptu and strategic, powerful and ethereal. As a result, the viewer is left with an infinite number of ways to interpret and respond to these artistic quilts.

Chiaki Dosho. *Reflecting Fish in the Sea,* 2004. Japanese antique *Tsumugi* silk, polyester, wool, yarn, paper, cording: 70 × 87 in. (178 × 220 cm). Machine corded, machine pieced, machine quilted. *Photo by D. Akasaka.*

Tsumugi silk is handcrafted using the same techniques that have been used for the past 400 years. The entire quilt top is made with blue and green *Tsumugi* silk, then covered with cording in a way that creates movement reflecting the waves of the sea and schools of fish shimmering in the light.

The creative cording sewn on the quilt top to create a sense of movement. *Photo by Akinori Miyashita.*

CHIAKI DOSHO lives in Kanagawa Prefecture, an area adjacent to the metropolis of Tokyo. The bustling Shinyurigaoka station near her home has a fairly large shopping mall with dozens of restaurants. People move quickly in every direction.

A short drive away, Chiaki lives in a high-rise apartment building. Once you step inside her quiet space, you immediately recognize that the studio is a reflection of her gentle personality. It is filled with beautiful wood antique furniture, everything from a stunning dining room table to a gorgeous antique chest filled with tools, fabric, and the like.

Her sewing table holds a large Bernina sewing machine and every other inch of it is covered with some useful tool, ribbon, thread, or fabric. She has sliding glass doors that lead to a small balcony where she can get a breath of fresh air or catch the warmth of the sun. On one wall, there is room to display one of her contemporary quilts, and near the ceiling she has installed a modern hanging system, so the quilts can be changed out easily.

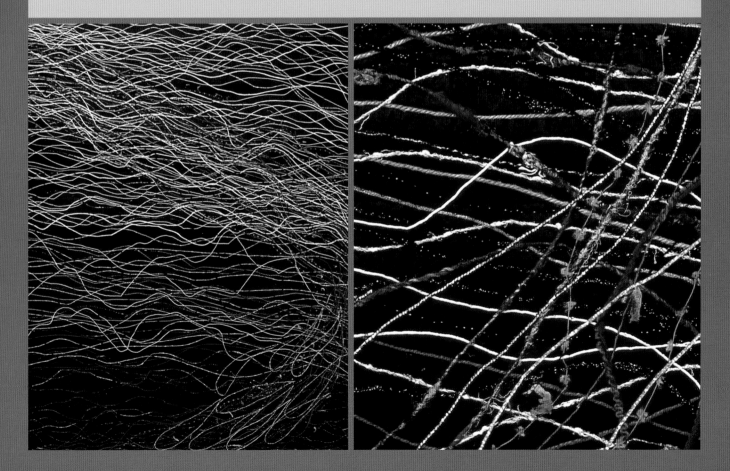

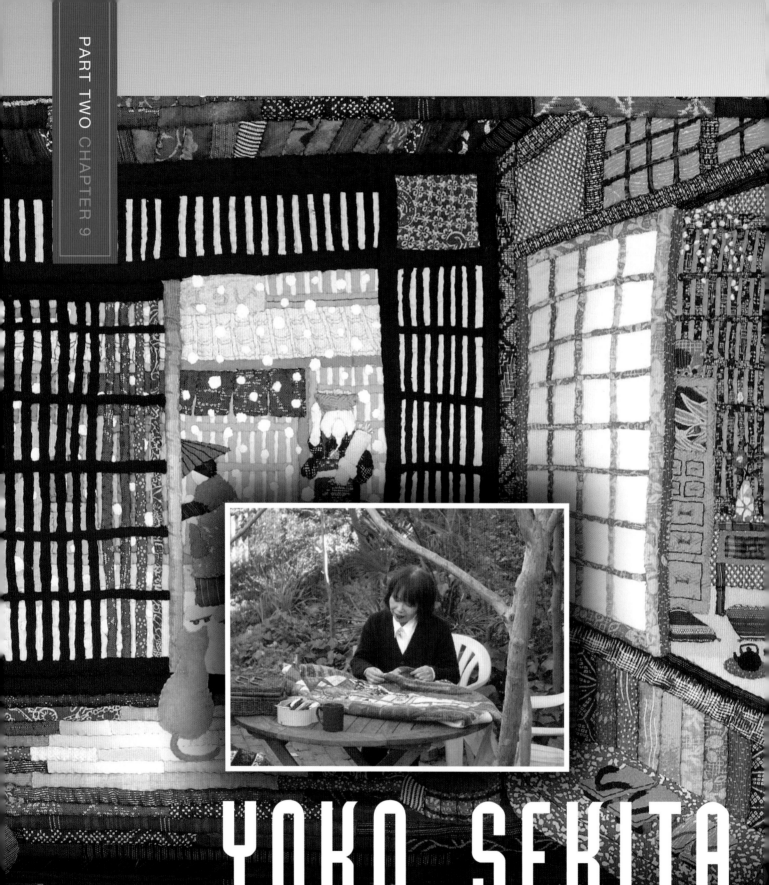

YOKO SEKITA
Telling Stories through Textiles

FROM MANGA ARTIST TO QUILTER

Yoko Sekita. *Kana Kana Mori*, 2008.
Cotton: 61 × 75 in. (157 × 190 cm).
Hand appliquéd, hand quilted.

Kana Kana is one of several "songs" sung by cicada insects each summer. *Mori* is
the term for forest. Yoko has recreated a sumptuous forest from her childhood
memories. The little girl in the middle is surrounded by a myriad of fairytale
characters as dusk descends on her and the cicadas begin to sing.

Yoko Sekita's story has a quintessentially Japanese beginning. She began her career as a cartoonist and illustrator for the Japanese manga *Margaret*. During the seven years she spent in this field, she became a popular cartoonist.

Manga is a sophisticated form of graphic novel (or cartoon). *Margaret* is a popular series in the *shōjo* genre, which is written primarily for young girls.

If there is one thing consistent in Yoko's entire body of art quilts, it is this central story of the traditions and everyday life of adolescent girls growing up in Japan, which is played out over and over in her quilts.

FROM HOBBYIST TO GRAND PRIX WINNER IN JUST A FEW YEARS' TIME

Yoko Sekita is one of those rare artists who can communicate an entire story through her textiles.

Yoko made her first quilt in the 1990s. She attended a quilt exhibition sponsored by a Japanese publisher and her world was forever changed. She was captivated by what quilters were doing with textiles and she immediately thought she could do the same.

In 2008, she won her first major award in a quilt competition, the Grand Prix award at the Tokyo International Great Quilt Festival. Since then, her quilts have been shown in galleries and exhibitions in Japan, the US, and Europe, and have been published in many magazines.

She is a self-taught quilter, learning entirely by trial and error. No classes. No books. No patterns. She also works entirely by hand, and she does so without the benefit of a dedicated studio. Yoko's studio is simply wherever she quilts, whether it is her garden or a corner of her home.

Like many self-taught artists, some of her technical skills are naïve, simply because she has figured out her own way of doing things. Every quilt she makes has some form of appliqué, and most have hundreds if not thousands of characters, houses, trees, and animals. This density of appliqué, all of which is edge-turned and hand sewn, is actually one of her trademarks.

Today, she continues to bring her unique point of view and her rich storytelling to create incredibly detailed village scenes loaded with characters in the midst of everyday life, and most of these characters seem quite happy.

When you study these tiny appliquéd humans and dogs, cats, and other animals, you may compare her quirky, whimsical style to paintings of Pieter Bruegel the Elder made in the late 1500s. Bruegel depicted his peasants in pubs, towns, and farm scenes. While many of his sixteenth-century paintings are considered masterpieces today, at the time his subjects and his depictions of everyday peasant life were unexpected imagery to glorify in art.

South Wind Bustling by Yoko Sekita depicts a German village and country folk engaged in a multitude of activities. There are so many engaging characters doing so many different things in this quilt, that it can easily be compared to the things depicted, at least, in Bruegel's *Netherlandish Proverbs* painting from 1559 which is densely populated with many engaging village folk.

In Yoko's art quilt, which was inspired by a trip she and her family made to Germany, some of the villagers are cleaning house, others are making beer or sausage, some are musicians performing in the village square, a drum corps marches through town, vegetables and other food are set out for sale, banners and flags hang from nearly every roof, and there is even dancing while an old woman sits in a rocking chair with her grandchildren nearby.

The painstaking difficulty of rendering each of these thousands of objects in cloth makes the end result all the more impressive.

Yoko Sekita. *Great Day to Be Busy*, 2009. Cotton:
59 × 74 in. (150 × 188 cm). Hand appliquéd,
hand quilted.

Another quilt rich in storytelling is *Kana Kana Mori*, which was created in 2008. There is a lone little girl set deep inside a dark but alluring forest. She is basking in a yellow-orange light, and outside her cocoon, the rest of the world is a happy, green, fairy-tale forest.

The title of this quilt holds cultural meaning to the Japanese. *Kana kana* is known as one of several "songs" sung by the cicada insects each summer. Some Japanese are especially attuned to the constant sounds of these creatures, and can differentiate their songs based on the time of year and the time of day. *Mori* is the term for forest. Japanese children are taught that the forest is magical and they often go out into the forest to play until they hear the *kana kana* song, which typically begins at dusk, and indicates that this is the time they should return home.

The little girl in this quilt stands in the middle of a magical world as she hears the *kana kana*, while fairy tales swirl all around her. Peter Pan, the Cheshire Cat, Alice in Wonderland, Mary Poppins, and other original characters—such as alien creatures playing string instruments and a tiny Leonardo da Vinci painting the *Mona Lisa*—are appliquéd on top of multiple layers of blue and green trees, leaves, a little house, even a castle.

Traditional Japanese homes and special holidays are also topics Yoko brings to life through her art. The traditional holiday *Hinamatsuri*, also known as Doll's Day or Girls Day, is held March 3. On this occasion, families display dolls dressed in traditional costumes in their homes. This is expertly depicted in one of her intriguing quilts.

In another titled *Snowy Day*, a little girl stands just outside the sliding doors of a traditional Japanese home. She is on her way out, while her cat sits and stares at her from the cozy warmth inside the house.

Yoko Sekita. *Let's Go to Market*, 2002. Cotton: 59 × 37 in. (135 × 95 cm). Hand appliquéd, hand quilted.

This lively market scene is densely packed with a multitude of characters, animals, stores, houses, and food and each detail is created by hand using only needle and thread.

In other quilts, it's not just girls, but entire villages and families depicted in lively settings such as the circus, the market, spring festivals, or the home, and each scene is filled with thousands of tiny appliquéd and embroidered details.

There are so many interesting moments in each scene that one can't help but want to move in close, and step inside these worlds. Each character is unique and is doing something different. There are even dishes and food on the dinner tables. Cats, birds, and even children linger inside the trees.

These worlds tell a story and—whether the setting is Japan, or Germany, or New York City—the story is both jubilant and timeless.

Besides the villages and country houses, another theme dominant in Yoko's work is the symphony orchestra. Yoko plays the piano and her affinity for music is lovingly expressed in artistic ways, but these musical stories also have moments of humor and whimsy.

In 2002, she created *Symphony No. 9* in which a joyous orchestra is performing Beethoven's Ninth Symphony on stage. In the background at the top of the quilt are fireworks in muted, beautiful orange tones. In the foreground, nearly every instrument is depicted in meticulous detail. The faces of the singers and musicians are all distinct.

But perhaps the most intriguing aspect is the sheer fun that plays out on the stage. Strewn about are musicians crawling around on the floor picking up sheet music, while others seem to be swaying with the music—especially the soloists whose arms are stretched out in song. Among the singers in the chorus, there are quite a few surprises: a chef singing, a man wrapped in bandages accompanied by his nurse, singers with beer mugs, a nanny with her baby. Among the orchestra, a couple of players have nodded off and another is peering down inside his neighbor's tuba. Among the soloists down in front, one is drinking wine, several appear to be locked in arms, and one has simply sat down.

This odd, quirky performance depicts the pure joy of experiencing Beethoven, and it certainly looks like a memorable concert.

Another musical quilt features a huge orchestra and is appropriately titled *Mischievous House of Music*. The same mix of joy and folly carries over to this one. One of the violinists has discarded his crutches and jumped up, the harpist appears to have fallen asleep, one of the trumpeters has raised his horn like a jazz player, and the percussionist is in a whirl. Better yet, some of the musicians seem to have simply wandered off and are depicted in the details in the top edges of the quilt.

To see this much happiness exuding from Yoko Sekita's creations is not really a surprise. Yoko believes that if the viewer sees something that the creator made with love and happiness, then those emotions will carry over to the work of art and, she hopes, will make the viewer happy for a moment as well.

She has also tackled more serious themes such as a recreation of the iconic Japanese original print titled *The Great Wave of Kanagawa*. The original was created by Katsushika Hokusai around 1830 and is known to many art lovers as simply as *The Wave*.

Yoko's version has layers of intricate quilting to capture the movement of the water. However, she has introduced a few new characters to the story. A tiny pirate is positioned off to the right of one wave, and a few folks who look as if they've just toppled out of their boat are lingering along the bottom border of the quilt.

Another historic story she has captured is *Scheherazade* (see front cover) and in her quilt the classic, captive Arabic storyteller lays longingly across the left side of quilt, her arm subtly draped amongst a flower and swirls of color. She appears momentarily at rest, her eyes clasped shut, seemingly exhausted from telling stories for a thousand and one nights. The choice of rich Japanese fabrics and vintage kimonos gives the queen a mysterious and unforgettable aura that is perfectly rendered with needle and thread.

QUILTS THAT EXUDE JOY AND HAPPINESS

Yoko Sekita. *Scheherazade*, 1994. Cotton: 36 × 41 in. (91 × 103 cm). Hand appliquéd, hand quilted.

"Scheherazade" is the ancient Persian story of a woman who tells a tale for 1,001 nights in order to captivate the king. For this quilted *Scheherazade*, Yoko has intertwined her figure with beautiful swirls of antique kimono appliqué. In the center, Scheherazade's hand dangles ever so gracefully.

BELOW
Yoko Sekita. *Mischievous House of Music*, 1991. Cotton: 70 × 43 in. (178 × 109 cm). Hand appliquéd, hand quilted.

A symphony orchestra performs on a stage filled with whimsy and moments of pure humor.

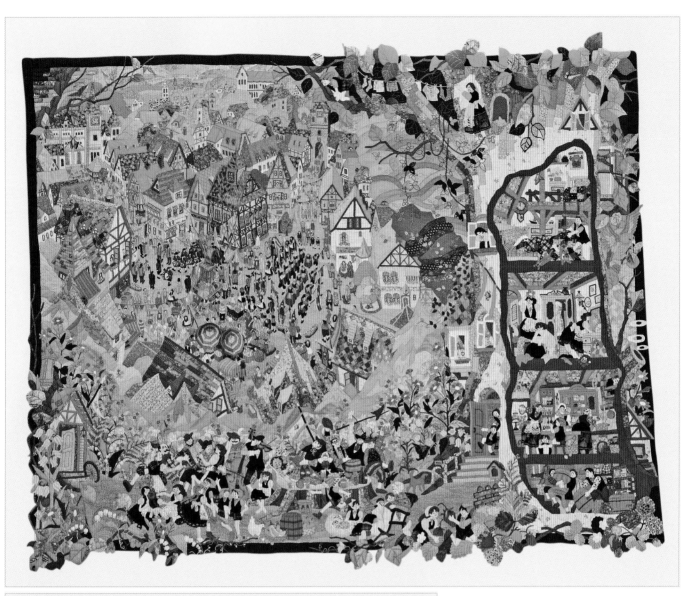

Yoko Sekita. *South Wind Bustling*, 1990. Cotton:
65 × 52 in. (164 × 133 cm). Hand appliquéd,
hand quilted.

The artist was inspired to make this quilt after
visiting a spring festival in Germany. She was
intrigued by the smell of beer and sausage cooking
mixed with the smell of spring flowers. Every inch
of this quilt is filled with tiny appliquéd details that
tell countless stories of life in this small town during
the first days of spring.

LEFT
Yoko Sekita. *Snowy Day*, 1998. Cotton: 20 × 15 in.
(52 × 39 cm). Hand appliquéd, hand quilted.

LEFT
Yoko Sekita. *Symphony No. 9,* 2002. Cotton:
28 × 74 in. (72 × 187 cm). Hand appliquéd,
hand quilted.

This art quilt conveys all that is magnificent about Beethoven's Ninth Symphony.
There are soloists in front, a full orchestra at center stage, and a chorus behind
them. Fireworks shoot off during the glorious moments of this piece of music.
Typical of Yoko's style, the performance also has a quirky side.

RIGHT
Yoko Sekita. *The Wave,* 2009. Cotton: 55 × 75 in.
(140 × 189 cm). Hand appliquéd, hand quilted.

Yoko Sekita. *Afternoon Sky*, 2001. Cotton: 36 × 41 in. (91 × 103 cm).
Hand appliquéd, hand quilted.

While village life is hustling all around, a young child climbs on the roof to
enjoy the red sky of an autumn afternoon.

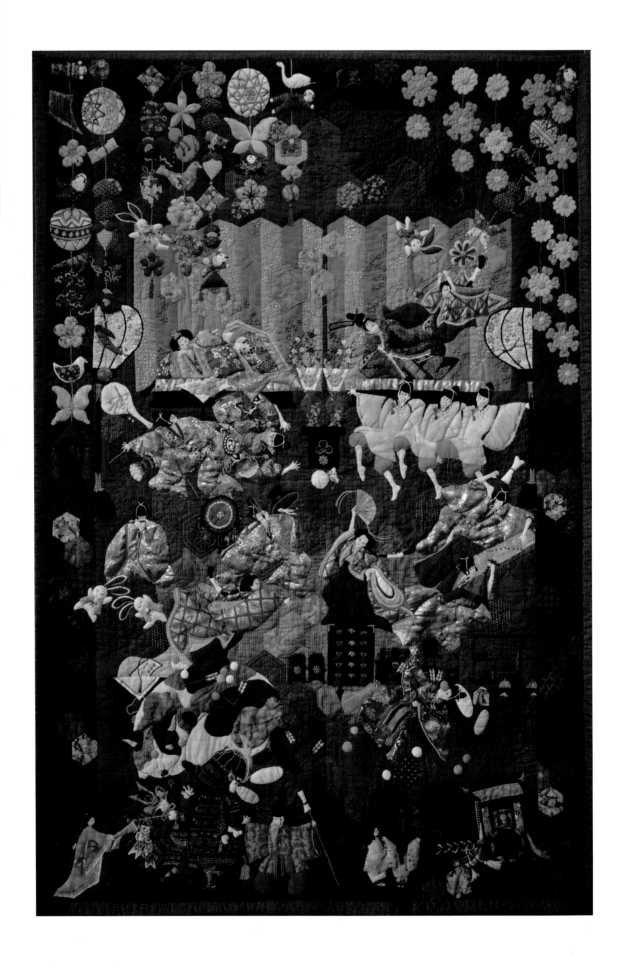

YOKO SEKITA does not have a dedicated studio. She is quick to explain that since she works entirely by hand, she is free to move from place to place, wherever she feels like working at that moment. Sometimes this is a small corner of her family room. Sometimes it is at the kitchen table. And sometimes she works in the beautiful garden outside her home in the suburbs of Tokyo. Yoko loves the freedom of not being tied to one place to work, and depending on where she is in her process, this flexibility is a huge advantage. When she needs to lay out her quilts and step back to take a look, the floor of the family room will do. If she needs to cut fabric and try out positions on the quilt top, she works in small doses on the closest table. And when she creates her hand-appliquéd figures and spends hours on hand quilting, she can do that just about anywhere.

OPPOSITE PAGE
Yoko Sekita. *Spring Midnight*, 2013. *Nishijin-ori* obi textiles, silk, cotton: 51 × 74 in. (130 × 188 cm). Hand appliquéd, hand quilted.

LEFT
Yoko Sekita. *Spring Midnight* (detail), 2013.

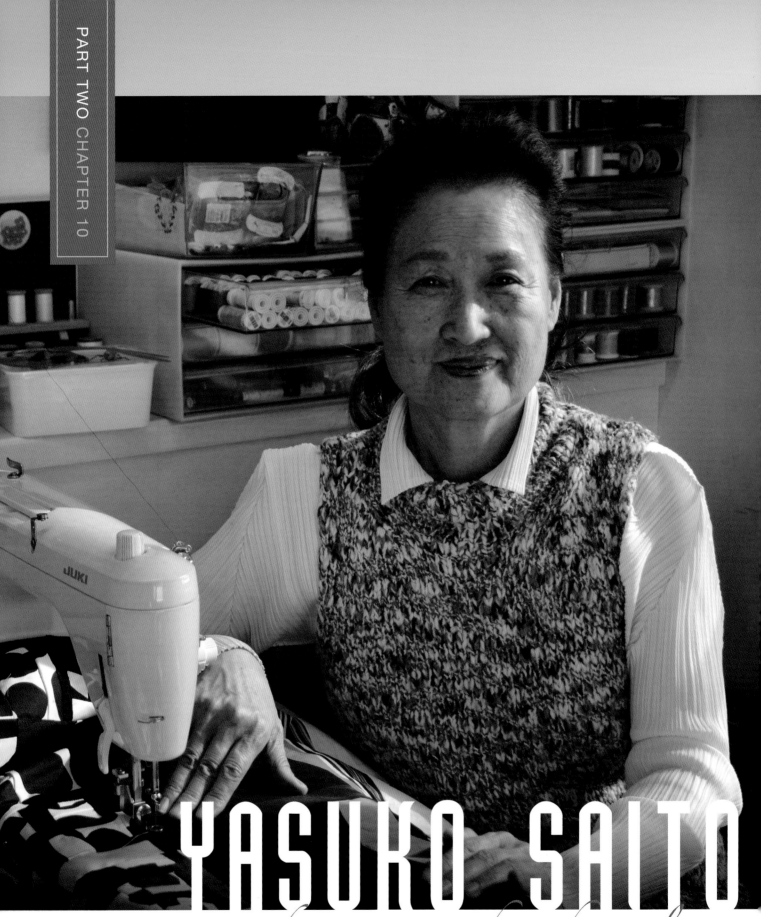

YASUKO SAITO

Innovation and Movement through Quilting

Yasuko Saito. *Movement #10* (detail), 2000. Silk, cotton, polyester, *washi*: 71 × 75 in. (180 × 190 cm). Painted, machine pieced, machine quilted. *Photo by Kazumasa Yamamoto.*

If there is one thing that Yasuko Saito would like her art to express most, it is movement. And this desire fits her personality as well as it fits her art.

Yasuko is high-energy and in seemingly constant motion. Keeping up with her means picking up the pace a bit.

As one might expect, with all this energy it's not unusual to find her working on six or seven quilts at once, all in varying stages of completion.

Every quilt she makes has curved, sweeping lines that create her hallmark sense of movement and she is a significant innovator in the way she pieces her quilts using a wide assortment of fabric, paper, and other textiles.

Yasuko is one of the active contemporary quilters in Japan who was not originally inspired by American antique quilts. She points out that her country has a 500-year history with textiles and that the nineteenth- and twentieth-century American quilts shown in Japan were too simplistic, too muted to be an inspiration to her quilting.

She did seek inspiration from contemporary American quilts, however, especially art quilts she saw when visiting the National Quilt Museum in Paducah, Kentucky, and at the Houston International Quilt Festival. During a subsequent visit to the US, she and a group of friends also traveled to the Dairy Barn in Athens, Ohio, to see Quilt National, an international exhibition.

She recalls that with each trip to America, she gained more awareness of contemporary quilts and as such, her eyes were opened to a whole new world.

Visiting these American exhibitions also encouraged her to begin entering domestic and international competitions herself. Yasuko's work was recognized at the very first Quilt Nihon competition in 1989–1990 and she has been included in many exhibitions since then. Her quilts are also in several private collections.

In 1999 and again in 2001, Yasuko's work was also accepted into Quilt National hosted in the US. Being selected for these two juried international competitions was a turning point for her career. Suddenly she began to think of herself as an artist with a career.

CLASSIC JAPANESE QUILT SCHOOL TRAINING

Yasuko Saito was an athlete in junior high and high school where she played volleyball. She continued playing volleyball in an amateur women's league for many years afterwards. She loved the exercise and the team spirit, but she felt she needed an additional outlet for her creative energy.

Like many of her contemporaries, she was originally a student of Hearts & Hands Patchwork Quilt School. She made her first quilt in the 1980s and she has hardly stopped to look back since then. She is always thinking about and planning her next quilt.

She also makes time to teach, and she's been teaching for more than ten years. She has about eight students who have been with her for years and she is extremely proud that one of her students won the grand prize at the Twelfth Quilt Nihon competition, which she considers a huge honor for her student. In addition, she is beginning to teach workshops internationally as well.

Her innovative use of materials is especially attractive to students wanting to expand into new possibilities for quilting. She is well-versed in mixing media, techniques which are somewhat novel in Japanese quilts.

Mixing *washi* (handmade paper) with traditional textiles is her specialty. The *washi* that Yasuko uses is a precious, artisan-made paper from the Kochi Prefecture, more specifically the tiny Shikoku Island, where this soft, yet durable paper is made much the same way it has been made for a thousand years. In fact, Shikoku is often referred to as the "Kingdom of Paper."

Yasuko will often cover parts of the *washi* with calligraphy, or other painted marks, before she tears it into smaller pieces and sews it together with her silk kimonos and other unusual fabrics, such as vinyl or gauze.

She also dyes her own fabric and purchases fabrics dyed to her exact specifications. This mixture of hard, soft, and inflexible textiles is difficult to combine seamlessly, but with skill and patience, she manipulates them to the exact form she envisions.

OPPOSITE PAGE, TOP TO BOTTOM
Yasuko Saito. *Movement #4* (detail), 1998. Cotton: 75 × 81 in. (180 × 205 cm). Painted, machine pieced, machine quilted.

Yasuko Saito. *Movement #20* (detail), 2002. Cotton, silk, linen, *washi*: 77 × 65 in. (195 × 165 cm). Painted, machine pieced, machine quilted.

Yasuko Saito. *Movement #68* (detail), 2013. *washi*, *Sumizome* dye: 13 × 23 in. (33 × 56 cm). Machine quilted.

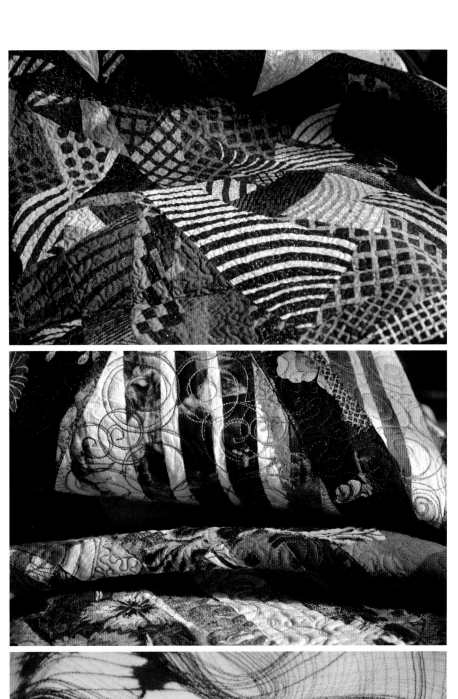

The results are bright, bold expressions. Some of her subjects are huge flowers, with one giant petal laid over another. Others have ribbons of fiber, or delicate free motion stitching, running through the entire image. And some of her more recent work is abstract; it is here where the unconventional material really shines.

It's unusual to see handmade paper sewn and quilted next to antique silk. And even though her designs are entirely contemporary, this use of traditional materials gives them an immediate sense of *wa*.

It is this combination that has also attracted the collectors who have purchased her work, some from as far away as Germany. Others are in Taiwan and Japan. She believes it is important, although admittedly difficult, for quilters to sell their work so that others can enjoy it. She believes that by selling her work and distributing it to others' hands, she is helping to preserve it as well.

The idea of trying to create a market for art quilts and encouraging fellow artists are the primary reasons that she founded the Japanese Contemporary Quilt Association in 2000. She serves as the group's chairperson and lends her energy to this group to keep its members up to date on quilt-related opportunities.

In 2005, the Japanese Contemporary Quilt Association held its first exhibition. Part of the mandate for this group is to create both professional networking opportunities and offer exhibition and contest entry opportunities for members, and Yasuko believes these efforts are gaining positive momentum.

It's no wonder that Yasuko has produced a whole series of quilts on the variation of movement. This is one quilter whose motion in real life—along with the motion she captures in her art—is ever-present.

Yasuko Saito. *Movement #25 Folding Screen*, 2004. Antique silk kimono, polyester, silk, gauze: 69 × 120 in. (175 × 304 cm). Machine pieced, machine quilted. *Photo by Kazumasa Yamamoto.*

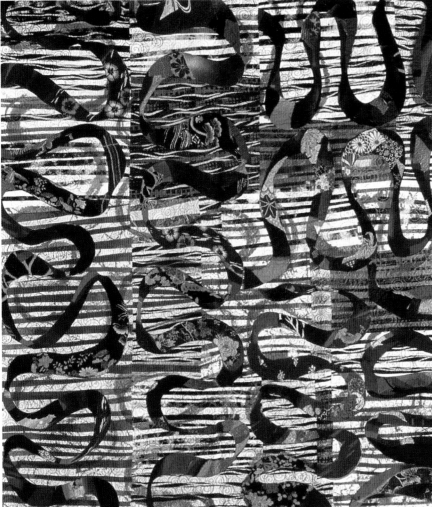

CLOCKWISE FROM TOP LEFT
Yasuko Saito. *Movement #29,* 2005. Silk:
81 × 91 in. (205 × 231 cm). Machine pieced,
machine quilted. *Photo by Kazumasa Yamamoto.*

Yasuko Saito. *Movement #10*, 2002. Cotton,
silk, polyester, *washi*: 71 × 75 in. (180 ×
190 cm). Machine pieced, machine quilted.
Photo by Kazumasa Yamamoto.

Yasuko Saito. *Movement #20*, 2002. Cotton, silk,
linen, *washi*: 77 × 65 in. (195 × 165 cm). Painted,
machine pieced, machine quilted.

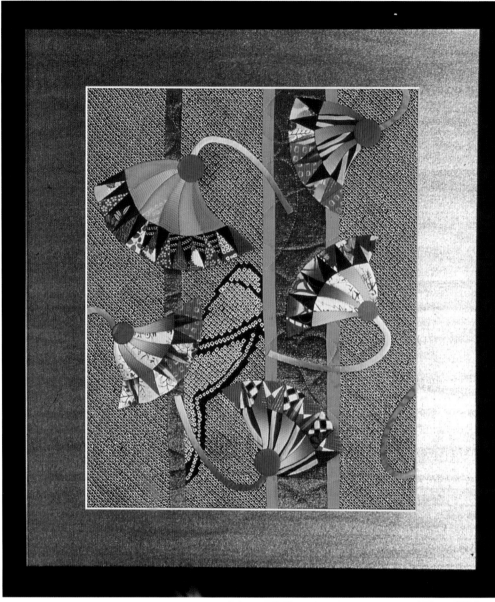

Yasuko Saito. *Wagaku-8*, 2003.
Antique silk kimono: 35 × 30 in.
(89 × 76 cm). Hand pieced, hand
quilted. *Photo by Kazumasa Yamamoto.*

RIGHT
Yasuko Saito. *Movement #26*, 2004.
Cotton, polyester, vinyl: 57 × 58 in.
(145 × 147 cm). Machine pieced,
machine quilted. *Photo by
Kazumasa Yamamoto.*

YASUKO SAITO'S studio packs a lot into a small space. Her studio sits on prime real estate, not far from central Tokyo, in a modern high-rise apartment building. Her kitchen, small dining table, and large sewing table make up the main room of the apartment and the large windows on two sides flood the room with light.

Just outside the main room, there is a huge closet—certainly large by Japanese standards—and this is where she stores her fabric, her special papers, her brushes, and her tools. Her finished quilts are professionally stored away in an amazingly organized fashion. Each quilt is carefully folded and stored in a soft-sided package, protected from light and dust.

The apartment has a warm, lived-in feel and everything is geared around the most important part of her daily life—creating art.

YOSHIKO KURIHARA
Figurative Fine Art
FROM PAINTING TO PATCHWORK

Yoshiko Kurihara. *Winter Story: Forlornness*,
2006. Cotton, lamé: 82 × 83 in. (208 × 210 cm).
Machine pieced, machine appliquéd, hand
embroidered, machine quilted.

Yoshiko made a series of quilts that draw upon the Japanese love of nature and the changing
seasons. In this one, three forlorn jesters stand in the cold winter snow. The center jester looks
at the viewer, arm raised and face blank, but the others look sad. The overall effect is strikingly
beautiful with snow that looks like magical stardust softly spread across these figures.

In 2006, Yoshiko Kurihara won the coveted and highly competitive Grand Prix award at the Tokyo International Great Quilt Festival. Even though she had won awards in other contests before that one, this particular honor took the self-taught quilter by complete surprise.

Yoshiko has formal training in fine art and oil painting, but her quilting techniques were learned outside the formal *iemoto* system. Traditionally, this scenario can make it more difficult to be accepted by the establishment, but Yoshiko felt a certain amount of confidence in her quilt and entered the competition.

She recalls that about a month before the results were announced, she received a call from the organizers. They asked a series of questions about her inspiration and her techniques. She assumed that they were trying to verify that her quilt, *Masquerade*, was original and therefore qualified to be in the competition. At the time, she had no indication this call was related to the Grand Prix award.

So when the results were announced, she was completely surprised and thrilled. This award marked a turning point in how she viewed her art, changing her mindset from hobbyist to artist. It also placed her firmly in the world of successful contemporary Japanese quilters.

FINDING HER MEDIUM

After graduating with a degree in fine art, Yoshiko worked in advertising for several years. She eventually got married and had children. Her first quilt followed the path of so many beginning quilters. When her daughter was young, she wanted to make her a quilted bedspread and doing so set her on an entirely new creative path.

As an oil painter, her art required intense amounts of time and space, something that was difficult in small Japanese homes, and the time required to paint was also difficult to find for a young mother.

With quilting however, she could work almost anywhere, in small increments of time, and she loved the challenge of trying to create images with textiles.

To this day, Yoshiko does not paint on her quilts, and she does not use hand-dyed fabrics. She feels that paint, even dye, is best saved for the canvas and if she wanted to work with paint, well then, she would paint instead of quilt. Instead, she loves the challenge of finding the exact color, texture, and pattern needed from fabric available in the retail market.

Her fabric collection is unusual in that it includes whole bolts of some of her favorite prints and solids. Her entire stash is neatly organized in her small space, arranged by color and collection.

Her fine art background also means she has formal training in both art and art history, and she was not inspired by the antique American quilts exhibited in Japan in the 1970s and 1980s. She was seeking a more contemporary and painterly effect with her quilts.

Her quilts are distinctive in the fact that all of them are figurative. Some of her characters are created on long panels that are then sewn together. Yoshiko loves the freedom that working in panels gives her; she is able to rearrange the characters in order to construct the overall image before the panels are connected.

Her figures range from fashionable young people out for a night on the town, to poignant court jesters, Renaissance-era circus clowns, and modern girls dressed in hats and sundresses either out for a summer stroll or surrounded by sunflowers.

The unifying traits of these characters are their strong geometric shapes and the lines the shapes create in the final piece.

One of the most stunning quilts in the collection is *Winter Story: Forlornness*. It features "Picasso-like" cubist court jesters who seem simultaneously merry and sad. Their faces, hands, and bodies are composed of variations of triangle and diamond shapes. One jester seems intensely interested in a snowflake, and the center jester looks straight at the viewer, arm raised as if he is in motion. The jester on the right is the most outwardly forlorn, and looks down, perhaps weighted down by the snow and ice of his world.

This quilt is created entirely by the pieced method, a technique that she feels is the only way to achieve the razor-sharp points that her geometric designs require.

Yoshiko starts with a fast sketch of her ideas. Then she converts this into a full-size technical drawing of her image. Next, this drawing is converted to graph paper and a pattern is made from that. Each pattern piece must be incredibly precise in order to fit together. Finally, the pattern is transferred to freezer paper, the pieces are cut out, and the search begins for the specific section of fabric with the color she requires.

Her work is recognized as much for this excellent piecing ability as it is for her lovely machine quilting.

That said, some quilts require appliqué, especially if she is going for a rounder, more natural quality. Her *Paris Café* quilt, which was on view at the 2014 Tokyo International Great Quilt Festival, is an example of one using appliqué.

Paris Café channels the round, elongated faces of Amedeo Modigliani to create an entire set of characters either sitting or serving at a very French café. The scene even offers art within art, featuring a "painting" on the back wall of the café. This quilted painting of a clown's face and collar is created with a modern batik fabric using both appliqué and a variation of reverse appliqué.

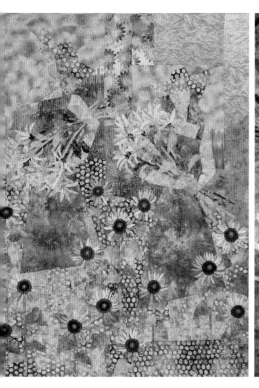

In the foreground of the café, three women face forward. Each is fashionably dressed and their detailed faces draw the viewer in immediately. These faces are intentionally left unquilted. There is also the back of a man's head as he shares a table with one of the women, and another gentleman is the server. He carries a bottle of wine and is wearing an apron with "café" spelled out ever so slightly with stitching.

Another quilt titled *Soleil: My Impressionism* is drenched with the yellow light of the sun. Two girls are incorporated into the design ever so subtly and they are surrounded by dozens of sunflowers. The girls, in their matching polka dot sun hats and delicate batik dresses, blend effortlessly with the bright decorative background fabrics.

The Impressionist effect Yoshiko was pursuing in this quilt is captured beautifully by combining people with nature, by joining a meticulously pieced quilt top with appliquéd and thread-embellished sunflowers, and by blending a collection of fabrics that perfectly mimics the yellow sunshine. One can't help but recall the poignant sunflowers of the post-Impressionist Vincent Van Gogh when looking at these compellingly quilted flowers.

LEFT
Yoshiko Kurihara. *Soleil: My Impressionism*, 2007. Cotton: 62 × 81 in. (57 × 205 cm). Machine pieced, machine appliquéd, hand embroidered, machine quilted.

The sun takes center stage in this beautiful, yellow summer scene. Yoshiko, inspired by the Impressionist landscapes, chose to create a bright summer day with beautiful sunflowers. Two girls in sundresses and polka dot sun hats are expertly pieced and so carefully placed in this scene that all the elements seem to melt perfectly together under the warmth of the sun. *Photo by Tsuyoshi Kurihara.*

RIGHT
Yoshiko Kurihara. *Soleil: My Impressionism* (detail), 2007.

Yoshiko Kurihara. *City: Summer*, 2006. Cotton: 71 × 83 in. (180 × 210 cm). Machine pieced, machine appliquéd, machine quilted. *Photo by Tsuyoshi Kurihara.*

BELOW

An example of the vibrant colors and intricate detail of Yoshiko Kurihara's art quilts. Many of her creations are pieced together, and it is difficult to achieve precise and sharp points using the piecing technique. The benefit of piecing versus appliqué in this case is a quilt top that is a perfectly smooth plane with impeccable points where desired. Yoshiko does employ appliqué methods on other quilts. All of them are expertly machine quilted.

Yoshiko Kurihara. *The Vanished Time of His and Mine*, 2005. Cotton: 69 × 87 in. (175 × 220 cm). Machine pieced, machine appliquéd, machine quilted.

This quilt was an exploration into a darker palette for Yoshiko. The figures on this black foundation are offset on neon panels. The quilt tells the story of the journey of love, from when couples meet and fall in love to their parting. Giant clock hands tick off time as the Roman numerals scatter outwards and several Dali-esque melting clocks remind us that time is fluid. *Photo by Tsuyoshi Kurihara.*

BELOW
Yoshiko Kurihara. *Dream*, 2010. Cotton, lamé, beads: 65 × 83 in. (165 × 210 cm). Machine pieced, machine appliquéd, hand and machine appliquéd, hand embroidered, machine quilted.

This quilt answers the question: "What kind of dream will the tired clown have after a long day at work?" It was honored with the Original Design Excellence Award at the 2011 Tokyo International Great Quilt Festival.

Yoshiko Kurihara. *At a Café—My "École de Paris,"* 2013. Cotton: 51 × 69 in. (129 × 175 cm). Machine pieced, machine appliquéd, hand appliquéd, hand embroidered, machine quilted.

The women at this café in the beautiful city of Paris resemble characters by French painter Amedeo Modigliani.

BELOW
Yoshiko Kurihara. *At a Café—My "École de Paris"* (detail), 2013.

Reaching this point of her career was a long road that covers more than 30 years of quilting.

In the early 1980s, Yoshiko's husband was transferred to Singapore, so she packed up her young family and moved from their home in Chiba City to the center of Singapore. At that time, there was only one quilt store in Singapore and the store's owner hosted a quilting bee. As Yoshiko joined this group of American, British, Scottish, Spanish, and Swiss quilters, she struggled to keep up with their conversations in English. However, she quickly made friends with the group and they bonded while sharing local tips on living in Singapore, information on schools, and even recipes. Being a part of this group not only expanded Yoshiko's quilting skills, it also improved her conversational English.

The next corporate move took them to Atlanta and after she settled in America, Yoshiko assumed it would be easy to join a guild.

QUILT BEES AND QUILT GUILDS STRETCHING FROM SINGAPORE TO ATLANTA TO NEW YORK

Yoshiko Kurihara. *The Scent of Summer,* 2008. Cotton: 62 × 86 in. (157 × 218 cm). Machine pieced, machine appliquéd, hand appliquéd, hand embroidered, machine quilted. *Photo by Tsuyoshi Kurihara.*

But it was surprisingly difficult to find the right group. She found her way to a local church group's quilting bee and the people she met there ended up being lifelong friends. The Atlanta quilting bee shared many activities that she enjoyed, and also helped build her creative and technical skills. The group made friendship quilts and regularly held challenge quilt events where members were encouraged to create new quilts on certain themes. These activities planted many creative ideas in her mind.

From Atlanta, the family moved again, this time to Rye, New York, just north of New York City. Finding a group of quilters here was significantly more challenging than it had been in Atlanta. In New York, most women were working, it seemed; plus, finding women who shared a love for quilting in this urban area was hard. She did finally locate a quilting bee, but these women were mostly making very traditional blocks and patterns.

Finally, the family moved back home to Japan and Yoshiko rejoined the quilt guild she had been a part of so many years earlier. When she did, she was able to share her international experiences with her new group. She showed them her friendship quilts from Asia and America, and she introduced the idea of challenge quilts. Both helped bring new creativity and energy to the group.

Yoshiko's quilts are works of art that have an enduring quality and international appeal, and the materials she uses to create them are widely available to quilters everywhere.

Because of her meticulous skills and pattern-making techniques, her trained eye, her sophisticated use of fabrics, and the choice of such figurative subject matter, these quilts can be definitely identified as artistic textiles from the hands of Yoshiko Kurihara—a quilter who is now firmly established in the world of contemporary Japanese quilts.

Yoshiko Kurihara. *Masquerade*, 2005. Cotton, lamé: 86 × 83 in. (218 × 210 cm). Machine pieced, machine appliquéd, hand appliquéd, hand embroidered, machine quilted.

This quilt was inspired by the musical *Phantom of the Opera*. It was named the Grand Prix winner at the 2006 Tokyo International Great Quilt Festival. *Photo by Tsuyoshi Kurihara.*

Chiba City is only about a 50-minute train ride from Tokyo, but the quiet streets make it seem a million miles away. **YOSHIKO KURIHARA** lives in a modest suburban home with her husband. The living area and kitchen are upstairs and the large dining table and comfortable family room are very warm and inviting.

The downstairs area has several rooms, and two of these are set aside for her studio: a tiny but tightly-organized sewing room, and a large traditional room next to it.

The small room has three small sewing tables, with a Brother sewing machine on each. The closet is filled with contemporary commercially-printed quilter's fabric, and some shelves are filled with entire bolts of fabric. Everything is impeccably organized.

The second room is a traditional Japanese-style room with *tatami* mats covering the floor. By day, Yoshiko can use this room to design her quilts, test out her fabric choices, or draw her large patterns. But at night, these things are easily moved away and futons are moved in, so the room can double as a guest room. The windows on the traditional sliding doors are covered in a thin white paper, creating a soft light inside the room. Her quilts are carefully stored in cardboard boxes, folded with tissue paper, and each one is clearly labeled, so any quilt can be located with just a moment of searching. Yoshiko's finished quilts are large, so this room is a critical part of her process—she needs space to study them and step back to gain perspective. And what better place to do so than in a lovely traditional Japanese room.

Yoshiko Kurihara. *Winter Story: Forlornness* (detail), 2006.

KEIKO GOKE

Color Galore and a Fresh Point of View

APPRECIATING THE UNCONVENTIONAL

Keiko Goke. *Tropical Seashore*, 1996. Cotton, no.
5 embroidery thread and sashiko thread: 79 × 64 in.
(200 × 163 cm). Hand appliquéd, hand pieced,
hand embroidered, hand quilted.

When you research the history of quilting in Japan, one name comes up over and over again: Keiko Goke.

Keiko made her first quilt in 1971 and ever since then, she has dedicated herself to creating one-of-a-kind, colorful textiles that exude her sense of optimism and joy, as well as her funky vibe.

To describe her style as individualistic, or in a class by itself, is an understatement. A better description comes from a dear friend who has known her for decades. She describes her in Japanese as "*heso magari,*" which translates literally as a "twisted belly button" and is used to refer to someone who is unique in every way.

Keiko Goke truly fits that description. And here's why.

She is a successful fabric designer with several lines of quilt fabric to her credit, she has authored a half-dozen books, and she has a following in Japan and all over the world. Basically she has a very successful quilt business, yet she has no staff and in no way does she consider herself a businessperson. She does not host an online store, and she does not operate a brick and mortar store. She admits that she only "plays the part of businesswoman" once a year for the Tokyo International Great Quilt Festival where she hosts one booth.

She is also a master teacher, yet she herself is completely self-taught. Based on her international success, she could command hefty teaching fees in Japan. Yet she charges very modest rates for her students who study with her on a regular basis, some of whom have been studying with her for decades. Her students prefer to think of her as a friendly coach and mentor, rather than as a master teacher.

In addition to teaching her quilt circle in Japan, Keiko occasionally teaches workshops in the US, Australia, New Zealand, Europe, and other locales.

INFLUENCE ALL AROUND

After high school, Keiko attended technical school to study illustration. It was during this time that she saw her first quilt printed in a publication. She immediately went to work trying to figure out how to make a quilt by looking at that one picture.

Later she would seek out pictures in quilt magazines, home decorating magazines, books, and other American lifestyle publications that might show quilts. When possible, she would cut these pictures out and keep them in a scrapbook.

There were no instructions of course, and at first, she didn't even realize a quilt had three layers of materials. She recalls that when she finally figured out there was a layer of batting in between the top and bottom fabric, she did not have those kind of supplies. So at first she improvised by using old towels or fabric for the inside.

Like most beginning quilters, she began by making traditional block quilts in the style of American quilts. She remembers attending those early museum shows of antique American quilts, including seeing the Holstein Collection of antique quilts when it was on view in Tokyo in 1975.

However, by this time she had already been making quilts for several years and while she thought the antique quilt shows were very well done, she found she was not influenced by these quilts because her sensibility was much more modern.

However, much later in her career she encountered vintage African-American quilts, and she credits these as being very inspirational to her art. She loved their sense of free-form, no-rules-required-quilting, and their bold use of color, and she sought out African-American quilts on trips to the US and in books.

More specifically, she was inspired by the wonderful collection of antique African-American quilts from the collection of Corrine Riley that were exhibited in Tokyo in 2007.

Long before that exhibition however, one of her most influential American experiences came in 1978 when she and a group of friends made their first trip to the United States. They visited both art and quilt destinations in New York City and Lancaster, Pennsylvania, then headed south to Houston, Texas.

Keiko Goke. *My Double Wedding Ring*, 2008.
Cotton: 88 × 87 in. (224 × 220 cm). Machine
pieced, hand embroidered, machine quilted.

When these young friends returned to New York to fly back to Japan, they were filled with new ideas, as well as books, patterns, and fabric for contemporary quilt making.

One of the primary lessons from this trip abroad, and the many others that followed in later years, was the concept of machine quilting as a means of expression. Keiko began machine piecing her quilts and using the machine to quilt in the 1980s, long before it was widely adopted by other contemporary quilters in Japan.

It was her early adoption of the sewing machine, plus her techniques and use of color, that garnered her considerable attention from judges, fellow quilters, and the media.

For example, Japan's national public broadcasting organization, NKK-TV, featured her in a segment on unique artisans early in her career. After the show was broadcast, she was told that many quilters who were working in traditional handwork ways were left saying, "Oh, you can't use a machine to make quilts." But they also wondered, "Or can you?"

USING COLOR TO CONVEY JOY, AND OFF-KILTER LINES TO CONVEY MOVEMENT

Over the years, there is one question Keiko Goke gets asked again and again: Where do you get your sense of color and how do you choose your colors?

It is a question she dreads, not because she does not want to answer, but because she cannot. Her color sense is simply innate. She cannot explain it.

Keiko does not plan out her quilts from start to finish. Rather she starts with an idea and then builds upon it little by little. The colors she uses pop up in her mind when she is ready to use them, and then she searches for the right fabric to fill her need.

Ironically, it was the times when she cannot find exactly the right fabric she needs that inspired her to design her own fabric lines. She designs and produces fabrics that appeal to her, and she doesn't think of what might sell, or be popular to others.

While she's fond of using her own fabrics in her quilts today, she also has a long history of incorporating traditional Japanese textiles into her quilts. One of her first quilts to receive international attention was titled *Indigo/Love/Me*, which she made in 1985 using traditional

Keiko Goke has always been one to think outside the box. This installation features a collection of quilted boxes—some of which are suspended in mid-air. Her characteristic brightly colored quilts are also hanging on the wall.

Keiko Goke. *Log Cabin in Wonderland I*, 1997. Cotton: 64 × 64 in. (162 × 163 cm). Machine pieced, machine quilted.

Keiko Goke. *Rob Peter to Pay Paul A*, 2008. Cotton: 70 × 70 in. (180 × 180 cm). Machine pieced, machine quilted.

Keiko used the idea of the traditional "Rob Peter to Pay Paul" block to make this quilt, only she chose to do so without the use of a pattern or ruler. The result is a fresh improvisational version of this vintage American classic quilt block.

kimonos and hand-dyed fabrics. This quilt was unusual in that some of the dyed fabrics were handcrafted by a woman who had been deemed a National Living Treasure by the Japanese government. Those fabrics were going to be discarded, and Keiko rescued them and made them into a quilt, thus preserving part of her heritage. (See page 43.)

A few years later, in 1988, she made a quilt that was inspired by a famous local festival known as the Tanabata Festival. The festival celebrates the myth of a female weaver and thus was attractive to Keiko. The date of the celebration is determined according to the lunar calendar.

Tanabata (which is pictured on page 11) is made with Japanese cotton, linen, and synthetic fabrics. She drew upon her childhood memories of the brightly-colored celebration to create an entirely new design that is both fresh and colorful.

Her design for *Tanabata* is actually made with a collection of large blocks, but the blocks are irregular, slightly off-kilter, and curve in different directions, which gives the quilt a great deal of movement. The use of Japanese fabrics and the reference to this mythological weaver, coupled with the joy of a starry, lunar festival, give it a very special sense of *wa*.

Perhaps it was this combination that drove curator Kei Kobayashi to choose *Tanabata* for the influential exhibition titled *Made in Japan: American Influence on Japanese Quilts*, which was exported from Japan and shown in several U.S. cities in 1990.

In 1997, she set about making a traditional log-cabin block quilt, yet true to her independent mindset, she did not use a pattern or ruler to make the blocks. Instead, she cut the pieces free-form and sewed them together in improvisational ways that referenced the log cabin, but also somehow seem very modern. In her quilt, titled *Log Cabin in Wonderland*, one can sense the strong influence of the improvisational piecing and colors of vintage African-American quilts.

The term "off-kilter" can be applied to so much of her artistic expression. Each one of her artworks, in its own way, takes the expected and gives it a slight twist.

I Wish We Could All Get Circular is a perfect example of this. In this quilt, Keiko is wishing the world would become a more peaceful place. She chose the circle because in Japanese culture, "to become round" means to mellow out, or be more peaceful. She made a whole series of circle quilts.

In this one, as in most of the others, of course the outlines of the circle design are a bit chaotic, which conveys movement and also can be interpreted to mean that the world is not yet peaceful. The chaos also makes the pattern infinitely more interesting.

Keiko Goke. *Cactus in Love*, 2002. Cotton: 66 × 66 in. (168 × 168 cm). Hand appliquéd, hand embroidered, machine quilted.

This whimsical cactus quilt kicked off a whole series of cactus quilts for Keiko. The inspiration came from a cactus in her garden outside her home in Sendai.

EVENTUALLY, ART EMERGES FROM THE 2011 EARTHQUAKE AND TSUNAMI

When the 2011 earthquake and tsunami struck northern Japan, the loss of life and the utter devastation had a huge impact on Keiko, and of course on many others. Her son and his young family lived on the East Coast and were forced to evacuate the area where the tsunami struck. They came to live with Keiko and her husband in Sendai, an inland city in the region, for several weeks.

In the days following the quake, there was no food, and other resources such as water and electricity were nonexistent. Trains and all other forms of transportation were not operating because the roads and tracks had been destroyed. No one could get in or out at first, and supplies quickly ran out. Keiko and her husband felt fortunate, though, because they were able to remain in their home, which was damaged but livable.

Naturally, quilting—and all art, for that matter—was shoved far away in order to focus on more important matters. But it was actually the renewal of life and hope after this tragedy that eventually brought Keiko back to quilting.

After many months, she receive a phone call from one of her students urging her to start teaching again, and she began to feel the time had come to resume her normal activities. But first, she felt it was important to see the area that was hit hardest by the earthquake and tsunami firsthand in order to try to process all that had happened. So Keiko and her husband made many visits to the coastline. What they saw, the utter destruction, was beyond comprehension. Everything had disappeared.

One day while visiting the area, she came across a handmade sign that had a poem written on it honoring the people who were lost. While reading this poem, her tears started to fall and at that moment she decided that one day she would make a quilt commemorating this beautiful poem.

As she and her husband continued visiting the area and talking with people who lived there, she noticed that new life was emerging. Flowers were blooming; she knew that life would continue. And she wanted to capture this poignant rebirth in art.

While it would be typical for some artists to turn to dark colors and dramatic themes to commemorate what this event meant to them, true to her individual style, Keiko chose to make art reflecting this event that is both bright and hopeful.

In 2012, she created a vivid, figurative quilt depicting a mother and child. The colorful bouquets of flowers, along with the mother and child, are symbolic of this new growth, new life, and hope for the future. The following year she made another quilt which she titled *People Who Became the Wind*. This art symbolizes the spirit of those who lost their lives and is an homage to the roadside poet she encountered on one of her first visits to the area. Through this artistic expression, Keiko wants show that the spirit of those who were lost will live on in the wind that surrounds us.

GIVING THANKS THROUGH QUILTING

The title of Keiko Goke's 2009 book, *All My Thanks and Love to Quilting*, sums up her viewpoint perfectly. She is an artist who has dedicated the past 40 years to bringing her artistic ideas to life through quilting.

Each new quilt, or series of quilts, offers a fresh perspective as well as bold color combinations and refreshing designs. Her style fits well in a modern, global quilting world where, like many quilters, she finds it can be difficult to trace her native roots.

Yet, with close inspection and an inquisitive exploration, the use of Japanese textiles and her own modern fabrics, coupled with her unconventional designs, help one to appreciate the *wa* factor in the art of Keiko Goke.

And for that, the quilting world also owes *her* a great deal of thanks and love indeed.

Keiko Goke. *Start from the Beginning*, 2001. American hand-dyed cotton: 60 × 62 in. (152 × 157 cm). Machine pieced, machine quilted.

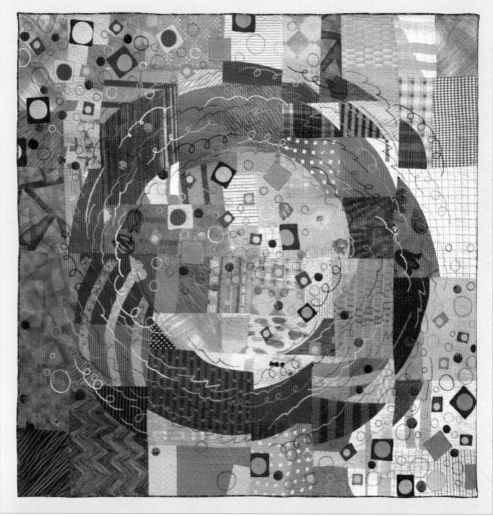

Keiko Goke. *I Wish We All Could Get Circular I*, 1999. Cotton: 70 × 70 in. (180 × 180 cm). Machine pieced, hand appliquéd, hand embroidered, machine quilted.

In Japanese, the expression "to become round" means to mellow out, or be more peaceful, and Keiko Goke has explored these ideas extensively in her art. For this quilt, she intends for the circle to represent the idea of a more peaceful place.

RIGHT
These giant quilted balloon balls are a demonstration of the creative expression that Keiko Goke brings to the art of quilting.

KEIKO GOKE lives in Sendai, in northern Japan. Her home is one of many homes in the region that suffered damage during the 2011 earthquake. Because Sendai is an inland city, it was spared the total destruction of large sections of the coast hit by the tsunami. To this day, Keiko and many others living in the region still suffer from fear, anxiety, and depression. When the earthquake struck, Keiko was at home alone, and she cannot forget the scene after the earthquake: everything in her studio was torn from its location. Books, fabric, tools, quilts were tossed around and piled on the floor in a huge mess.

At first, there was so much devastation and deprivation around the Sendai region and the East Coast of Japan that quilting was the farthest thing from her mind. Eventually, repairs were made, roads were cleared, trains started up, schools and businesses began operating, and life for Keiko began to feel normal again. She returned to making art and her showcase at the 2014 Tokyo International Great Quilt Festival marked a return to her signature brightly-colored world where all is well, people are happy, and life must continue.

BIBLIOGRAPHY

Baird, Merrily. *Symbols of Japan* (New York: Rizzoli, 2001).

Bishop, Robert, Karey Bresenhan, and Bonnie Leman. *Hands All Around: Quilts from Many Nations* (New York: E. P. Dutton, 1987).

Brandon, Reiko Mochinaga. *Country Textiles of Japan: The Art of Tsutsugaki* (New York / Tokyo: Weatherhill, 1986).

Bresenhan, Karey Patterson. *500 Traditional Quilts* (New York: Lark, 2014).

Cabinet Office of Japan. 2009 Public Opinion Survey on Diplomacy (courtesy of The Maureen and Mike Mansfield Foundation), http://mansfieldfdn.org/program/research-education-and-communication/asian-opinion-poll-database/listofpolls/2009-polls/cabinet-office-of-japan-2009-public-opinion-survey-on-diplomacy-09-35/.

Cang, Voltaire Garces. "Preserving Intangible Heritage in Japan: The Role of the *Iemoto* System." *International Journal of Intangible Heritage,* vol. 3, 2008, pp. 71–80.

Dresser, Christopher. *Traditional Arts and Crafts of Japan (1882)* (New York: Dover, 1994). Edition is an unaltered replica of the 1882 book published by Longmans, Green & Co., London, under the title *Japan: Its Architecture, Art and Art Manufacturers*.

Endo, Noriko. *Confetti Naturescapes: Quilting Impressionist Landscapes* (Worthington, OH: Dragon Threads, 2010).

Geis, Darlene, ed.; foreword by Robert Bishop and Elizabeth Warren. *The Quilt Encyclopedia Illustrated* (New York: Harry N. Abrams with Museum of American Folk Art, 1991).

Goke, Keiko. *All My Thanks and Love to Quilts: Art Quilts Created by Keiko Goke* (East Petersburg, PA: Design Originals, 2009). English language edition, 2012.

Hatano, Shoko. *My Contemporary Quilts* (Japan: Art Box/Akiyoshi Kizuka, 2003.)

Holstein, Jonathan. *Abstract Design in American Quilts: A Biography of an Exhibition* (Louisville, KY: The Kentucky Quilt Project, 1991).

Japan Handicrafts Instructors Association. *Japanese Imagery in One Hundred Quilts* (Tokyo: Japan Handicrafts Instructors Association and Kokusai Art, 2004).

Japan Handicrafts Instructors Association, foreword by Tadanou Seto. *One Hundred Japanese Quilts: An Exhibition of New Works by Quilt Artists in Japan* (Tokyo: Japan Handicrafts Instructors Association and Nihon Vogue Co. Ltd., 2004). This is the catalog of the exhibition that originated in Japan in 2002 and then traveled to the US and Europe, 2003–2004.

Kawamoto, Akio; foreword by Barbara Brackman. *Beauty in Japanese Quilts* (Tokyo: Kokusai Art, 1990).

Kida, Takuya. "Japanese Crafts and Cultural Exchange with the USA in the 1950s: Soft Power and John D. Rockefeller III during the Cold War," *Oxford University Press Journal of Design History,* 2012.

Kleiner, Fred S. *Gardner's Art through the Ages*, 14th ed. (Boston: Clark Beaver, 2011).

Kokusai Art. *Old and New Quilts from Ancient and Modern Cities* (Tokyo: Kokusai Art, 2007).

Kuroha, Shizuko and Penny Nii. "A Glimpse of the Japanese Quilting Community: The Influence of Quilting Schools," *The Quilt Journal* vol. 2, no. 2, 1993.

Liddell, Jill and Yuko Watanabe. *Japanese Quilts* (New York: E. P. Dutton, 1988).

Louie, Elaine. "Images of Japan, Ancient and Modern, Make an Old American Craft Seem New," *New York Times,* Mar. 13, 1991. Review of the exhibition *Made in Japan: American Influence on Japanese Quilts*.

McGray, Douglas. "Japan's Gross National Cool," *Foreign Policy* no. 130, May–June 2002, pp. 44–54.

Mingei International Museum. *Bold Expressions: African American Quilts from the Collection of Corrine Riley* (San Diego, CA: Mingei International Museum, 2011).

New England Quilt Museum. Catalog to accompany *Made in Japan: American Influence on Japanese Quilts* (Lowell, MA: New England Quilt Museum, 1990).

Nomura, Nao. "The Development of Quiltmaking in Japan since the 1970s," *Uncoverings 2010*: Volume 31 of the Research Papers of the American Quilt Study Group, 2010.

Onoyama, Takako. *Honoring the Seasons: Quilts from Japan's Quilt House Yama* (Hong Kong: That Patchwork Place, 1996).

Oxmoor House. *Big Book of Best-Loved Quilt Patterns* (Birmingham, AL: Oxmoor House/ Leisure Arts, 2002).

Peterson, Karin Elizabeth. "Discourse and Display: The Modern Eye, Entrepreneurship, and the Cultural Transformation of the Patchwork Quilt." University of California Press: *Sociological Perspectives* Vol. 46, No. 4 (Winter 2003), pp. 461–490).

Roberts, Elise Schebler. *The Quilt: A History and Celebration of American Art Form* (Minneapolis, MN: MBI Publishing and Voyageur Press, 2007).

Saito, Yoko. *30th Anniversary of Quilt Party* (Japanese edition) (Tokyo: Nihon Vogue Co., Ltd., 2008).

——. *Basket Made from Cloth* (French/English edition) (St. Etienne de Montluc, France: Quiltmania, 2010).

——. *Japanese Taupe Color Theory: A Study Guide* (First edition, Tokyo: Patchwork Tsushin Co., Ltd., 2009; English edition, Singapore: Stitch Publications LLC, 2013).

——. *Quilt Party 2004* (Japan: Quilt Party Ltd., 2004).

——. *Quilt Party 2010* (Japan: Quilt Party Ltd., 2010).

——. *Quilt Party 2011* (Japan: Quilt Party Ltd., 2011).

Shirane, Haruo. *Japan and the Culture of the Four Seasons* (New York: Columbia University Press, 2012).

Sielman, Martha. *People & Portraits: Art Quilt Portfolio* (New York: Lark Crafts, 2013).

Smucker, Janneken. *Amish Quilts: Crafting an American Icon* (Baltimore, MD: The John Hopkins University Press, 2013).

Surak, Kristin. "From Selling Tea to Selling Japaneseness: Symbols of Power and the Nationalization of Cultural Practices." *European Journal of Sociology,* 2011, vol. 52, no. 02, pp. 175–208.

Unger, Miles. "A New Member at the Quilt Bee." *Boston Globe*, July 1990. Review of the exhibition *Made in Japan: American Influence on Japanese Quilts*.

Yang, Sunny and Rochelle M. Narasin. *Textile Art of Japan* (Tokyo: Shufunotomo Co., Ltd., 1989).

Yasushi, Watanabe and David L. McConnell. *Soft Power Superpowers: Cultural and National Assets of Japan and the United States* (Armonk, NY and London: East Gate Books and M.E. Sharpe, 2008).